THE ACADEMIC EDGE LTD.

Physics Grade 12

Go Beyond Your Limits

ISBN: 1-55202-028-2

The Academic Edge Ltd.

Congratulations! You are obviously very interested in investing in yourself and becoming the best you can be. Our curriculum-based guides are supplemental learning aids that provide uncomplicated and straightforward explanations, examples, exercises, solutions and practice tests.

The study guides are intended to assist you, the student, in understanding key concepts and in developing the necessary skills that will enable you to achieve maximum results in school or government exams. Combined with classroom instruction, reading and practice received from your school resources, these guides will be an invaluable asset in achieving your academic goals.

The Academic Edge Ltd. commissioned experts in their specific areas to develop our study guides. The mandate is to provide useful guides that are curriculum specific to offer you an alternative resource – a study companion that will enhance your efforts. **"A personal tutor in a book".**

Challenge yourself to "GO BEYOND YOUR LIMITS"

The Academic Edge Ltd.

The Academic Edge Ltd.
7090 Brentwood Drive
Brentwood Bay, B.C.
V0S 1A0
1-800-403-4751

About the Author:

Robert Vaudan obtained his Bachelor of Education degree from the University of Alberta, majoring in mathematics and physics. He has taught for many years in public and private schools in Alberta.

For the past 10 years, he has been Science Department Head at St. Lukes College in Edmonton. He has also occupied the vice-principleship position there as well. He currently teaches math and physics at the College.

By being aquainted and knowledgeable in math, Mr. Vaudan integrates mathematical concepts into his physics lessons, so that students can see how to use mathematics in the analysis of the physical world.

His math and physics classes have succeeded in Physics 30 and Math 30 with class averages well above the provincial average. He is a well-respected educator held in high esteem by students, parents, peers, and administration.

He hopes that you will find this study guide useful, and that his explanations of Physics 30 concepts will allow you to be better at physics. The better you get at it, the more you will enjoy it, and you too can join those elite students who have gone before you, and thoroughly enjoyed physics.

If this is the vision of the future; if this is the direction in which we want to move. Well then, we next have to decide what we are going to do to get it done. Visions are not self fulfilling. We cannot stand idly by and expect dreams to come true on their own power.

The future is not a gift it is an achievement.

Robert F. Kennedy, 1968

PHYSICS GRADE 12

This study guide is intended to assist students of high school physics in understanding key concepts and developing the necessary skills that will enable the student to achieve maximum results on government diploma exams. It is not intended to replace classroom instruction, nor the reading of text books. It could be used to supplement these.

The guide is written in the simplest terms, and divided into the following basic parts.

1- Necessary Mathematics

2- Physics 11 Review

3- Conservation Laws

4- Electricity and Electric Fields

5- Magnetic Fields and Electromagnetic Radiation   Physics 12

6- Radioactivity

It is recommended that you read over the entire unit. Try the problem set at the end of each unit after reading the solutions to the problems that are solved for you. You should then have the necessary basic understanding of physics concepts to help you solve any problems that you may face on exams, or in question sheets given to you by your teacher! Good luck and enjoy your physics!

PHYSICS GRADE 12

Table of Contents

PHYSICS GRADE 12

PHYSICS GRADE 12

PHYSICS GRADE 12

Necessary Mathematics

The Metric System

As mathematics is the tool used by Physicists to analyze the physical world, some basic mathematics is necessary in any study of physics. Since measurements of measurable quantities is often required, we begin our study with a review of the **metric system** of measurement (This system is often called the SI system). **Standard** or **basic units** are used to measure length, time and mass.

Length has a basic unit of **meters**. (abbreviated m)

Time has a basic unit of **seconds**. (abbreviated s)

Mass has a basic unit of **kilograms**. (abbreviated kg)

The size of the units is determined by interchanging prefixes followed by a **root** word (**meter**, **second**, or **gram**). Since the system is based on powers of 10, it is necessary to know these powers.

$$10^1 = 10 \qquad\qquad 10^{-1} = 1/10 = 0.1$$

$$10^2 = 10 \times 10 \qquad\qquad 10^{-2} = 1/10 \times 1/10 = 0.01$$

$$10^3 = 10 \times 10 \times 10 \qquad\qquad 10^{-3} = 1/10 \times 1/10 \times 1/10 = 0.001$$

etc. etc.

There are many prefixes, but you should be familiar with the following major units.

kilo (k)	10^3	centi (c)	10^{-2}
mega (M)	10^6	milli (m)	10^{-3}
		micro (μ)	10^{-6}
		nano (n)	10^{-9}

PHYSICS GRADE 12

1 Mm is 1 megameter and this means 10^6 meters or 1 million meters.

1 cs is 1 centisecond and this means 10^{-2} seconds or 1 one-hundredth of a second.

6 µg is one microgram and this means 6×10^{-6} grams or 6 millionths of 1 gram.

I find that in dealing with high school physics these rules should be followed when working with the metric system.

1- Since the system of measurement used is primarily the mks (meter-kilogram-second) system, *convert* all units when problem solving to meters, kilograms, and seconds.

2- Memorize the powers of ten that correspond to the common prefixes.

      To do a conversion is simple.

<u>8 Mm expressed as meters is</u>   Since M is 10^6, then 8 Mm is 8×10^6

8×10^6 m   meters.

<u>15 µs expressed in seconds is</u> 15×10^{-6} s.

15×10^{-6} s

PHYSICS GRADE 12

Scientific Notation

You will often work with very large or very small numbers, so you should be able to express measures using scientific notation. A number is in this form when it is expressed as

$$M \times 10^n$$

M is always a number 1 or greater, but always *less than* 10. Therefore $1 \leq M < 10$.

n is a power of 10 and is an **integer**. An integer is a **whole number** that is positive or negative. Although n could be 0 or 1, these two integers are rarely used. a number like 526 could be written as

$$5.26 \times 100$$
$$= 5.26 \times 10^2 \quad \text{correct scientific notation form.}$$

A number like 0.000327 could be written as

$$3.27 \times \frac{1}{10,000}$$
$$= 3.27 \times 10^{-4}$$

Certain rules can be used to express measures in scientific notation.

Every number has a **decimal point** that separates whole units from part units.

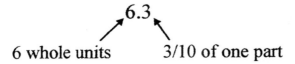

6 whole units   3/10 of one part

> **Rules:**
>
> 1- Move the decimal behind the first digit that is not a zero.
>
> 2- Count the number of positions that the decimal has been moved to the *left* or *right*.
>
> 3- This number is the power of ten when the number is written in scientific notation.

Examples: Express each number in scientific notation.

1) 34, 800   Note that the decimal is here 34, 800.

Move the decimal behind the 3 so

34, 800.

The decimal is moved 4 places towards the left. When the decimal is moved left the power is + (positive)

Therefore $34, 800 = \mathbf{3.4800 \times 10^4}$.

Notice that $M \times 10^n = 3.4800 \times 10^4$

M is a number between 1 and 10.

n is a whole number.

When I see a number like 3.4800×10^4, I know that the decimal should be 4 decimal places to the right for the actual number.

3.4800×10^4

move 4 decimal places to the right

34, 800.

PHYSICS GRADE 12

2) 0.000059

To write this number in scientific notation, move the decimal behind the 5 (rule 1). Note that the decimal moved 5 places to the right.

$$0.000059 \qquad \text{so M} = 5.9$$

Since the decimal was moved right, the power of 10 is - (negative)

$$0.000059 = \mathbf{5.9 \times 10^{-5}}$$

When I see a number like this I know that this is a *very small* quantity. (The negative power tells me this)

3) 17 million = 17 000 000

$$= 17\ 000\ 000.$$

$$= 1.7\ 000\ 000 \qquad \text{move decimal left 7 positions}$$

$$= \mathbf{1.7 \times 10^{7}}$$

4) 4 thousandths = 0.004

$$= 0.004. \qquad \text{move decimal right 3 positions}$$

$$= \mathbf{4 \times 10^{-3}}$$

5) mass of automobile

$$4326\ \text{kg} = \mathbf{4.326 \times 10^{3}\ kg}$$

6) mass of flea egg

$$m = 0.00069\ \text{g}$$

$$= \mathbf{6.9 \times 10^{-4}\ g}$$

Note: to convert this mass to *kilograms* multiply by conversion factor:

$$1 \text{ kg} = 1000 \text{ g}$$

$$1 \text{ kg} = 10^3 \text{ g}$$

therefore
$$6.9 \times 10^{-4} \text{ g} \times \frac{1 \text{ kg}}{10^3 \text{ g}} \quad \text{(g units cancel)}$$

$$= \frac{6.9 \times 10^{-4}}{10^3} \text{ kg}$$

$= 6.9 \times 10^{-4} \times 10^{-3} \text{ kg}$ (this step is explained in the

$= \mathbf{6.9 \times 10^{-7} \text{ kg}}$ next section of this unit)

7) mass of the Earth (very large)

$$5\ 980{,}000{,}000{,}000{,}000{,}000{,}000{,}000{,}000. \text{ kg}$$

24 positions left (+)

$= \mathbf{5.98 \times 10^{24} \text{ kg}}$

7) mass of an electron (very small)

$$0.0000000000000000000000000000911 \text{ kg}$$

31 positions right (−)

$= \mathbf{9.11 \times 10^{-31} \text{ kg}}$

PHYSICS GRADE 12

Laws of Exponents

Multiplication and Division

Scientific notation is used to simplify calculations and write very large and small numbers in short form. To multiply or divide, remember these rules.

Exponent rules:

1) $a^m \times a^n = a^{m+n}$ 'a' is the base

m and n are the exponents.

example: $10^6 \times 10^5 = 10^{6+5} = 10^{11}$

2) $a^m \div a^n = \dfrac{a^m}{a^n} = a^{m-n}$

example: $10^6 \div 10^5 = \dfrac{10^6}{10^5} = 10^{6-5} = 10^1$

3) $(a^m)^n = a^{m \times n}$

example: $(10^2)^4 = 10^{2 \times 4} = 10^8$

These laws allow us to do rapid calculation when multiplying or dividing numbers that are expressed in scientific notation.

Examples:

1) $(2 \times 10^6)(3 \times 10^7) = 2 \times 10^6 \times 3 \times 10^7 = 2 \times 3 \times 10^6 \times 10^7$

$= (2 \times 3) \times (10^6 \times 10^7)$

$= 6 \times 10^{6+7}$ (same base: combine and add exponents)

$= 6 \times 10^{13}$

---

2) $(4.6 \times 10^8)(3.9 \times 10^{-4})$ $= 4.6 \times 3.9 \times 10^8 \times 10^{-4}$

     $= 17.94 \times 10^4$ use calculator   add in head $= 8+(-4)$

but this answer is not in the correct scientific form.

but we know that

     $17.94 = 1.794 \times 10^1$

therefore $17.94 \times 10^4 = (1.794 \times 10^1) \times 10^4$

                   $= 1.794 \times (10^1 \times 10^4)$

                   $= 1.794 \times 10^5$ is the correct form

3)

$$\frac{(7.5 \times 10^6)(4.3 \times 10^9)}{(8.3 \times 10^7)} = \frac{7.5 \times 4.3}{8.3} \times \frac{10^6 \times 10^9}{10^7}$$

               do on calculator   use laws of exponents

     $= 3.886 \times 10^{6+9-7}$

     $= 3.886 \times 10^8$

Addition and Subtraction

When adding or subtracting numbers written in scientific notation, the one rule to remember is that the exponents of 10 must be equal before adding or subtracting.

Examples:

1) $(5.2 \times 10^3) - (4.1 \times 10^3) = (5.2 - 4.1) \times 10^3$

     same exponents (3)

         $= 1.1 \times 10^3$ (easy to do)

2) $(4.5 \times 10^3) - (5.1 \times 10^2)$

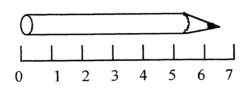

       not the same

not so easy now. We must move the decimal in one number to make exponents equal before we can subtract. (usually change the smaller exponent to the larger)

Therefore $5.1 \times 10^2 = (0.51 \times 10^1) \times 10^2$

                  $= 0.51 \times 10^{1+2}$

                  $= 0.51 \times 10^3$

Now

    $(4.5 \times 10^3) - (0.51 \times 10^3)$ subtraction can now occur

    $= (4.5 - 0.51) \times 10^3$

    $= 3.99 \times 10^3$

These rules apply equally to addition.

Significant Digits

Accuracy in measurements depends upon the instrument that is used to make the measurement. For example: If you measure the length of your pencil using a ruler that shows centimeters as the smallest units marked off, you may measure the pencil as follows.

It is *at least* 6 cm long, but *not quite* 7 cm long. Therefore a measure of *about* 6.5 cm would be a reasonably good measure.

But if the millimeters were marked on the ruler

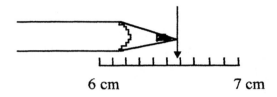

6 cm   7 cm

A measure of 65 mm is too short, but 66 mm is too long. A measure of 65.8 mm would be the best measure.

Notice that in both cases we *estimated* the final digit as *tenths* of the smallest unit on the measuring instrument. **In science it is always assumed that the last digit of any measure is a good guess**.

Addition and Subtraction

      Now if we were to add or subtract measurements, there is some uncertainty (last digit is a guess) in each measure. So, for example, if we were to add 6.5 mm + 4.29 mm

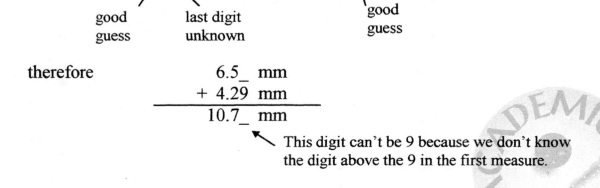

therefore

$$
\begin{array}{r}
6.5\_ \text{ mm} \\
+ \ 4.29 \text{ mm} \\
\hline
10.7\_ \text{ mm}
\end{array}
$$

This digit can't be 9 because we don't know the digit above the 9 in the first measure.

10.79 mm

Is this number significant ? That is, is this a useful part of the sum ? Since it is *probably* incorrect, we round the number off.

10.8 mm would be the best answer for this sum.

The rules to remember when adding or subtracting measures are;

1- line up the decimal points.

2- put question marks in unknown positions.

3- round off digits where question marks appear above.

Example: 4.2 cm + 5.693 cm + 7.48 cm = _____

```
   4.2??   cm
   5.693   cm
   7.48?   cm
  17.373   cm
      ↑↑
```

not significant because of ? above, **round off**.

= 17.4 cm

If the first digit that is not significant is 5 or greater, add 1 to the last significant digit. If less that 5, drop off and add nothing.

Multiplication or Division

Expressing answers to the correct number of significant digits when multiplying or dividing *depends on the number of significant digits of each measure used in the calculation.*

PHYSICS GRADE 12

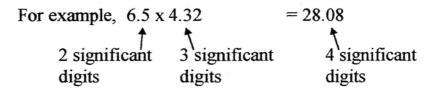

For example, 6.5 x 4.32   = 28.08

2 significant   3 significant   4 significant
digits   digits   digits

> **Rule:** The answer when multiplying must be rounded to the least number of significant digits of the measurements used in the calculation.

For this example   2 sig. digits x 3 sig. digits = _____ 2 sig. digits

so the best answer to   6.5 x 4.32 = 28

2 sig.   3 sig.   2 sig.
digits   digits   digits

> **Rules for determining the number of significant digits in any measurement:**
>
> 1 - All non-zero digits are significant.
>
> examples: 432 seconds has 3 significant digits
>
> 6.249 m has 4 sig. digits
>
> 82.639 kg has 5 sig. digits (All digits are important including the last digit which is a good guess).
>
> 2- Zeros between non-zero digits are significant.
>
> examples: 5002 km has 4 sig. digits
>
> 6.0039 mm has 5 sig. digits
>
> 10.506 cm has 5 sig. digits
>
> 3- Zeros at the end of a number are significant.
>
> examples: 6.40 g has 3 sig digits
>
> 15.98000 mm has 7 sig. digits

1500 km has 4 sig. digits (A measure like 1500 km is an exact number and these can often be thought as having *any* number of significant digits; 1500 has 4 sig. digits

1500.0 has 5 sig. digits

1500.00 has 6 sig. digits)

4- Zeros at the beginning of a measure are *not* significant.

examples: 0.8 mm has 1 sig. digit

0.0039 km has 2 sig. digits

5- Exact numbers are treated as if they have any number of sig. digits.

example: If 8 people each get 4.6 pies, how many pies are needed ?

Since 8 is exact and 4.6 pies has 2 sig. digits, then treat 8 with sig. digits. Therefore

$$8.0 \times 4.6 = 36.8 \text{ pies} \qquad \text{round to 2 sig. digits}$$

$$= 37 \text{ pies (answer expressed to 2 sig. digits)}$$

PHYSICS GRADE 12

Units

In physics, units are always given with measurements. Units, used correctly can;

1) be used to derive new units

2) be used to check your work

3) be used to determine formulas

1) All units are **basic** or **derived**.

Basic units: In physics 20 and 30 we use

1- meter (m)

2- kilogram (kg)

3- second (s)

4- Ampere (A)

All other units are derived from these basic units.

For example: velocity is measured in $\dfrac{m}{s}$

acceleration in $\dfrac{m}{s^2}$

force in Newtons (N) $1\,N = 1\dfrac{kg \cdot m}{s^2}$ **basic units**

work in Joules (J) $1\,J = 1\,N \cdot m = 1\dfrac{kg \cdot m^2}{s^2}$

power in Watts (W)

$$1\,W = 1\,\frac{J}{s} = 1\,\frac{N \cdot m}{s} = 1\,\frac{\frac{kg \cdot m^2}{s^2}}{s} = 1\frac{kg \cdot m^2}{s^3} \quad \text{etc.}$$

Necessary Mathematics

PHYSICS GRADE 12

2) If, for example, you are calculating energy and energy must be measured in Joules, carry units through your calculations.

Example: Kinetic energy = 1/2 (mass)(velocity)²
A 2.2 kg mass has a velocity of 12.3 m/s, what is its K.E. ?

Since $m = 2.2$ kg and $v = 12.3$ m/s, then

$$KE = \frac{1}{2}mv^2$$

$$= 0.5(2.2 \text{ kg})(12.3 \text{ m/s})^2$$

$$= 0.5(2.2 \text{ kg})(151.29 \text{ m}^2/\text{s}^2) \qquad \text{notice units are}$$
$$\text{squared}$$

$$= 0.5(332.838 \; \frac{\text{kg} \cdot \text{m}^2}{\text{s}^2}) \qquad \text{combine units}$$

$$= 0.5(332.838 \; \frac{\text{kg} \cdot \text{m}}{\text{s}^2} \cdot \text{m})$$

$$= 0.5(332.838 \; \text{N} \cdot \text{m}) \qquad \text{-N is a derived unit}$$

$$= 0.5(332.838 \; \text{J}) \qquad \text{-J is a derived unit}$$

$$= 166.419 \; \text{J} \qquad \text{-are the units correct ?}$$
$$\text{if yes, probably done}$$
$$\text{correctly)}$$

$$= \underline{\hspace{2cm}} \qquad \text{-think significant}$$
$$\text{digits ?}$$

2.2 kg has 2 sig. digits and 12.3 m/s has 3 sig. digits. 2 is the least number of significant digits, therefore answer should be expressed to 2 sig. digits.

PHYSICS GRADE 12

170 J has 3 sig. digits, so use scientific notation to
express as 2 sig. digits.

that is **1.7×10^2 J is the best answer**.

3) If velocity is measured in $\dfrac{m}{s}$ ⟵ distance or displacement

⟵ time

therefore

$$\text{velocity} = \frac{\text{displacement}}{\text{time}}$$

$$v = \frac{d}{t}$$

here's the formula. I know it's correct because of the units.

or

$$\text{force} = \text{mass} \times \text{acceleration}$$

$$= (kg) \times (m/s^2) \ \text{units}$$

$$= \frac{kg \cdot m}{s^2}$$

$$= \text{Newtons}$$

If I know that: $\quad 1 \ N = 1\dfrac{kg \cdot m}{s^2}$

$$1 \ N = 1 \ kg \ (m/s^2)$$

units of force = units of mass (units of acceleration)

so $\qquad\qquad F = ma \qquad$ here's the *formula*!

PHYSICS GRADE 12

Relationships Between Variables (Variation)

Physicists are very interested in determining the relationship that exists between two variables:

We will encounter 3 main types,

1) Linear (Direct)

2) Parabolic

3) Inverse

Simple Example: If an object travels at a constant speed is there a relationship between the distance traveled and the time required to travel ?

An experiment is devised to collect data concerning the variables of *distance* and *time*. The experimenter controls one variable - the **independent** or **manipulated** variable. The measure of the second variable will **depend** upon the measure of the first. The second variable depends on the first. Therefore it is called the **dependent** or **responding** variable. For example, the experimenter may measure the distance after *each hour* of travel. Therefore the experimenter will first measure time and then measure distance.

The following data is obtained.

Time (hr)	0	1	2	3	4	5
Distance (km)	0	60	120	180	240	300

PHYSICS GRADE 12

When this data is examined, you can see that doubling the time doubles the distance, tripling the time triples the distance, etc. We say there is a **direct** or **linear** relationship existing between the two variables. The data may be plotted on a **graph**. The graph will tell us quickly the type of relationship that exists between the variables.

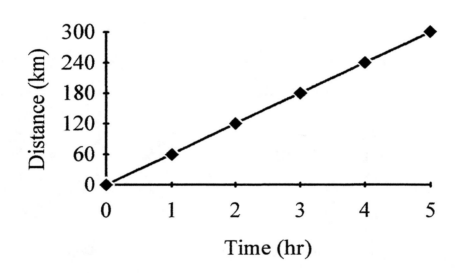

Distance vs. Time

Rules for Graphing:

1- Independent variable is always placed on the x-axis. This is controlled by the experimenter. Dependent variable is always on the y-axis.

2- Label each axis and show appropriate unit used.

3- Use a **scale** on each axis so that all the data values can be plotted

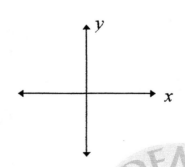

Necessary Mathematics

PHYSICS GRADE 12

4- Units on the scale should be correct

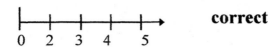 **correct**

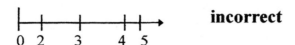 **incorrect**

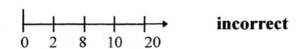 **incorrect**

5- Measures will sometimes be slightly off. Do not 'connect the dots'.

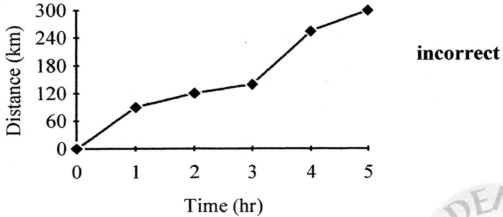 **incorrect**

instead find a *line* (straight) that best *fits* the data

PHYSICS GRADE 12

Distance vs. Time

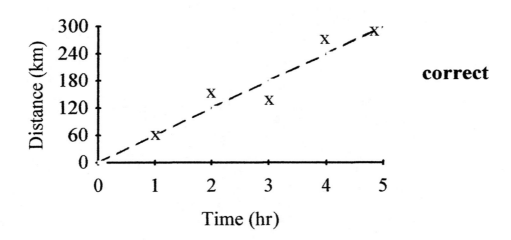

correct

Some data points may be 'off' the line. Try to set the same number of 'off dots' on both sides of the line. A *straight line* graph indicates a direct or linear relationship. Using variation we can write

$$y \propto x \qquad \text{'}y \text{ varies directly as } x\text{'}$$

This means that if x doubles, then y doubles at the same time. This relationship can then be written in mathematical form.

$$y = k\,x$$

k is a proportionality constant.

k will always be the slope of the line.

To find the **slope;**

in math:
$$m = \frac{y_2 - y_1}{x_2 - x_1}, \qquad \text{where } m = \text{slope}$$

(x_1, y_1) are coordinates of one point *on* the line, and (x_2, y_2) are the coordinates of another point *on* the line.

---

y vs. x

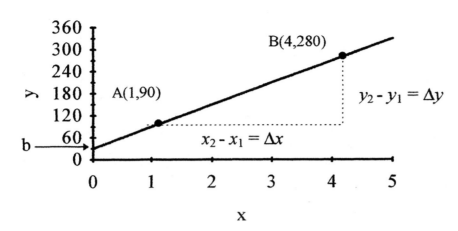

$A(1,90) = (x_1, y_1)$

$\text{slope} = m = \dfrac{y_2 - y_1}{x_2 - x_1} = \dfrac{\Delta y}{\Delta x} = \dfrac{\text{rise}}{\text{run}}$

$B(4,280) = (x_2, y_2)$

$m = \dfrac{280 - 90}{4 - 1} = \dfrac{190}{3} = 63.3$

$y \propto x$

$$y = mx + b$$ is the linear equation of every straight line in slope (m) y-intercept (b) form. If the line passes through the origin (0,0) then b=0 and the equation is

$$y = mx.$$

Notice that the proportionality constant k = slope "m".

Therefore, in our example:

$$m = \frac{\Delta y}{\Delta x} = \frac{60 \text{ km}}{1 \text{ hr}} = 60 \text{ km / hr}$$

$y \propto x$

and   distance $\propto$ time   direct relationship indicated

$d \propto t$ ←———   by straight line graph.

$d = k \cdot t$ ←———   mathematical equation
(y=intercept is 0)

---

since k = m then,

$$d = (60 \text{ km/hr})t$$ is the equation that can be used to predict any d at any given t.

6- Title your graph

The title is always **Dependent vs. Independent**

variable on y-axis   versus   variable on x-axis

Types of graphs indicate different relationships

1- **Linear** (always a direct relationship)

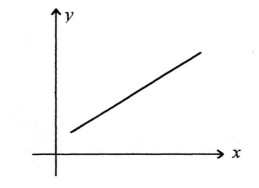

$$y \propto x$$

$$y = kx$$

2- **Parabolic** (direct but "y to x^2")

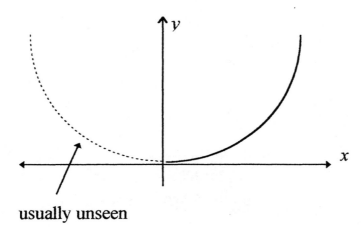

usually unseen

When you see a graph like this, then $y \propto x^2$ (y varies directly as x^2)

$$y = kx^2$$

To find k, plot y vs. x^2

Sample data

x	0	1	2	3	4	5
x^2	0	1	4	9	16	25
y	0	5	20	45	80	125

y vs.x   y vs.x^2

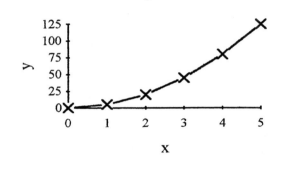
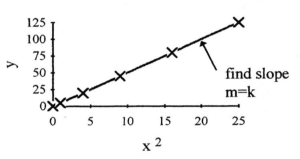

find slope
m=k

3- **Inverse** : Graph is always a hyperbola

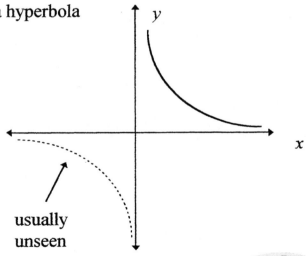

usually
unseen

Sample data

x	1	2	3	4	5
y	100	50	33.3	25	20

PHYSICS GRADE 12

As x increases, y decreases. $y \propto \dfrac{1}{x}$

$$y = \dfrac{k}{x} \qquad \text{k is always "yx"}$$

Variables in any equation can have their relationships determined easily.

For example, $F_g = \dfrac{Gm_1 m_2}{R^2}$

In this equation;   G is a constant

$F_g \propto m_1$ As m_1 increases F_g increases directly.
double m_1 will double F_g..

$F_g \propto m_2$ As m_2 increases F_g increases directly

also.

$F_g \propto \dfrac{1}{R^2}$ As R increases F_g will decrease (inverse

relationship).

Another example: $F = ma$

$F \propto m$ tripling the mass triples the force.

$F \propto a$ tripling the acceleration triples the force.

$$m = \dfrac{F}{a}$$

$m \propto F$ if a is constant, then F and m vary

directly.

$m \propto \dfrac{1}{a}$ if F is constant, then a and m vary

inversely.

Relationships will be refreshed periodically throughout the workbook.

PHYSICS GRADE 12

Trigonometry

Right Triangle Trigonometry(Math 10)

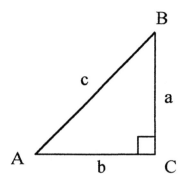

$$\sin A = \frac{a}{c} = \frac{opp}{hyp}$$

$$\cos A = \frac{b}{c} = \frac{adj}{hyp}$$

$$\tan A = \frac{a}{b} = \frac{opp}{adj}$$

Oblique Triangle Trigonometry(Math 20)

No right (90°) angles.

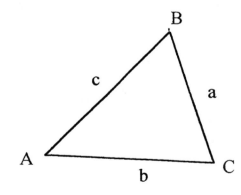

Law of Cosines

$$a^2 = b^2 + c^2 - 2bc\cos A$$

$$b^2 = a^2 + c^2 - 2ac\cos B$$

$$c^2 = a^2 + b^2 - 2ab\cos C$$

Law of sines

$$\frac{a}{\sin A} = \frac{b}{\sin B} = \frac{c}{\sin C}$$

PHYSICS GRADE 12

Use the law of sine and cosine to solve oblique triangles when given certain information.

Information Given:

A=Angle
S=Side

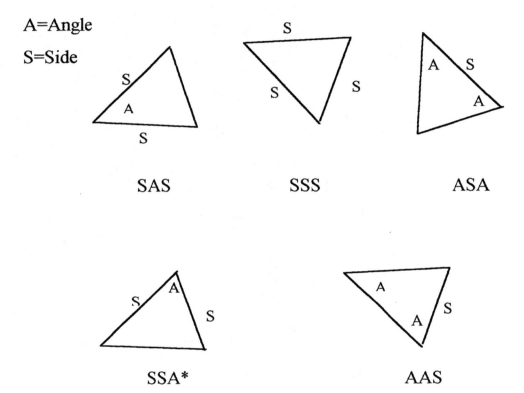

SAS   SSS   ASA

SSA*   AAS

* sometimes more than 1 triangle can be drawn from the given information: CAREFUL!

For SAS and SSS use the law of cosines.

For ASA, SSA*, and AAS use the law of sines.

You now have the necessary skills and math to proceed with physics. The next unit will review major concepts from Physics 20.

Physics 11 *Review*

The following unit presents *key* concepts from the current Physics 20 curriculum that are required to succeed in Physics 30.

Vectors

In physics some measured quantities are **scalar quantities**, and others are **vector quantities**. A scalar quantity has a certain **size** or **magnitude** only. A vector quantity has a **direction** as well as a **size** or **magnitude**.

	scalars	vectors
1	distance	displacement
	example: 10 meters	example: 10 meters East
2	speed	velocity
	example: 50 km/hr	example: 50 km/hr North
3	time	acceleration
	example: 5 hours	example: 5 m/s^2 West
4	energy or work	force
	example: 10 Joules	example: 33 Newtons to the right

and others

Scalar quantities can be added together algebraically

Vector quantities must be added geometrically.

PHYSICS GRADE 12

Example: A man walks 10 m East and then 15 m North.

a) What distance did he walk ? 10 m +15 m = **25 m**

b) What was the man's displacement ?

      To answer this question, we must use a **vector diagram**. Vector quantities are represented by arrows drawn in the correct direction and to an appropriate scale.

      Standard directions are;

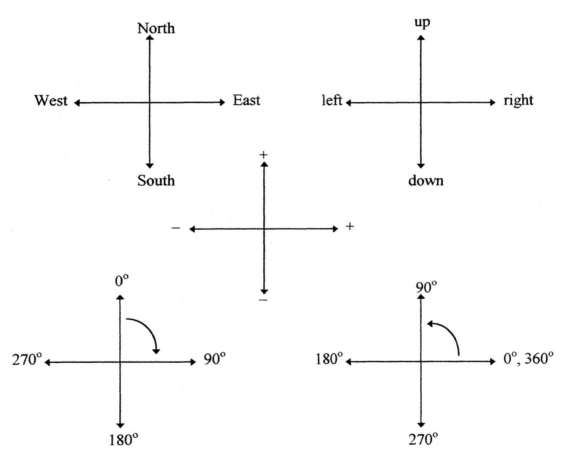

Navigation	**Mathematics**
True North is 0° and directions are expressed in angles rotated *clockwise* from True North	Here, the + x-axis is the assigned 0° and angles are measured by rotations *counterclockwise* from the positive x-axis.

PHYSICS GRADE 12

Direction are always expressed from a **reference point**. If point A is our

reference point then   A
                        ●

place a coordinate plane (x and y-axis) with 'A' at the origin.

A North-East direction from A is then shown as an

arrow pointing in the appropriate direction.

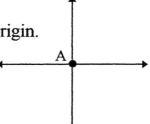

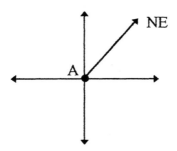

A vector has a **head** and a **tail** end.

tail
end

head
end

Now, a vector of 10 m East can be represented by a vector (arrow) drawn

in the eastern direction.

10 m east

A vector of 15 m North can be drawn as

If we want to find the sum of 10 m East and 15 m

15 m north

North, we first draw vector 1 and then vector 2 starts

from where vector 1 ends. Draw each vector in the correct direction.

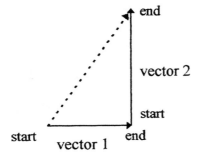

The sum is a third vector drawn from

the tail of the first vector to the head

of the second vector. This vector is

often called the **resultant**. The

dashed line represents the sum of the

two vectors. The magnitude of the sum is best determined mathematically, using trigonometry or Pythagoras' Theorem.

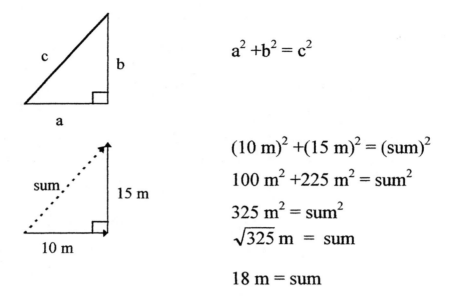

$$a^2 + b^2 = c^2$$

$$(10 \text{ m})^2 + (15 \text{ m})^2 = (\text{sum})^2$$

$$100 \text{ m}^2 + 225 \text{ m}^2 = \text{sum}^2$$

$$325 \text{ m}^2 = \text{sum}^2$$

$$\sqrt{325} \text{ m} = \text{sum}$$

$$18 \text{ m} = \text{sum}$$

The direction is determined by trig.

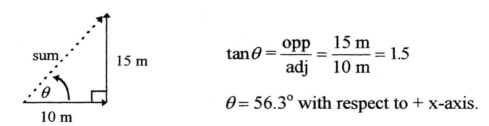

$$\tan\theta = \frac{\text{opp}}{\text{adj}} = \frac{15 \text{ m}}{10 \text{ m}} = 1.5$$

$$\theta = 56.3° \text{ with respect to + x-axis.}$$

An important idea concerning vectors is that *any* vector quantity can be represented by vector diagrams (arrows in correct direction), and any vector can be described as the sum of two perpendicular vectors called **components**.

1)

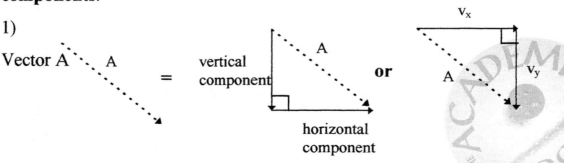

PHYSICS GRADE 12

2)

Vector B

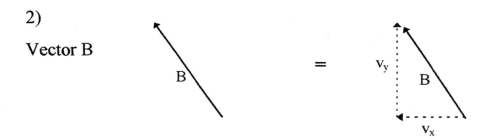

Since any vector is the sum of two perpendicular components, the two components are independent of each other. For example: a bee has wings that can give it a velocity in a certain direction. If the wings stop, then a blowing wind may give the bee a velocity in a different direction. The bee will have a resultant velocity that depends upon both vectors.

For example:

> vector A: velocity of 10 m/s North given by wings.
>
> vector B: velocity of 20 m/s West given by wind.

If only wings used,

> v = velocity = 10 m/s North

If only wind blowing

> v = velocity = 20 m/s West

If both wings and wind are used, then the velocity of the bee is the sum of the two vectors.

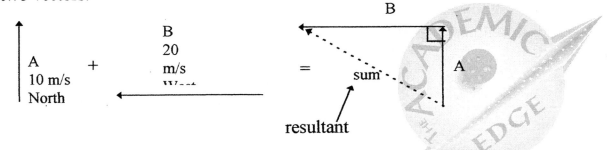

by Pythagoras

$$\text{sum}^2 = (10 \text{ m/s})^2 + (20 \text{ m/s})^2$$
$$= 100(\text{m/s})^2 + 400(\text{m/s})^2$$
$$= 500 \ (\text{m/s})^2$$
$$\text{sum} = \textbf{22 m/s North West}$$

The important idea here is that every second the wings carry the bee 10 m North ($v = 10$ m/s North), but at the same time the wind carries the bee 20 m West. Therefore the bee moves North-West.

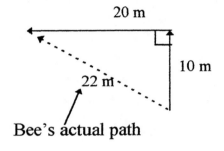

Bee's actual path

PHYSICS GRADE 12

Kinematics

This branch of physics uses mathematics to analyze **motion**. Key words are **displacement**, **velocity**, **time**, and **acceleration**. Often **distance** and **speed** are used when direction is not important for displacement and velocity.

When an object maintains a "more or less" **constant velocity**. we use

vectors → $v_{ave} = \dfrac{d}{t}$ ← (velocity$_{average}$=displacement/time)

scalars → $v_{ave} = \dfrac{d}{t}$ ← (speed$_{average}$ = distance/time)

but more often objects accelerate (chage their velocity)

$$a = \frac{\Delta v}{t}$$

often we use v_i = initial velocity (before change occurs)

v_f = final velocity (after change occurred)

then

$$a = \frac{v_f - v_i}{t}$$

In high school physics all accelerations are uniform, meaning that velocity changes equal amounts during equal time units. An acceleration of 10 m/s^2 means that the velocity is changing 10 m/s for each second that the acceleration occurs, or

a = 10 m/s per second

From rest at

t=0 s	v=0	
t=1 s	v=10 m/s	speed increases 10m/s
t=2 s	v=20 m/s	per second
t=3 s	v=30 m/s	

therefore a = 10 (m/s)/s or 10 m/s^2.

While an object is **accelerating** in a straight line

$$v_{ave} = \frac{v_f + v_i}{2}$$

since $d = v_{ave}\,t$, then

$$d = \left(\frac{v_f + v_i}{2}\right)t$$

to find displacement while accelerating.

Since from

$$a = \frac{v_f - v_i}{t}$$

$$v_f = v_i + at$$

then by replacement

$$d = v_i t + \frac{1}{2}at^2$$

Also since

$$t = \frac{v_f - v_i}{a}$$

then by replacement

$$d = \frac{v_f^2 - v_i^2}{2a}$$

or

$$v_f^2 = v_i^2 + 2ad$$

By using the above equations, motions in a straight line can be analyzed. Which equations to use depends upon the information given and the quantity that you want to determine.

PHYSICS GRADE 12

Dynamics

This branch of physics deals with "why objects move". Of course, they move because of **forces**. Forces are explained as a **push** or **pull** that an object experiences. Since they act in certain directions, forces are vector quantities.

An important force is the force of gravity (F_g). This force acts between every two masses. It is always a force of attraction. Therefore two masses, free of all other forces, will exert pulls on each other and move together. The formula to calculate this force is

$$F_g = \frac{Gm_1 m_2}{R^2}$$

where G = universal Gravitational constant
  = 6.67 x 10^{-11} Nm^2/kg
  m_1 = mass #1 (measured in kg)
  m_2 = mass #2 (measured in kg)
  R = distance separating the masses measured from centre to centre (expressed in meters)

Usually, the force is so small that it is insignificant. This is if m_1 and m_2 are small masses. But if one of the masses is large, like the Earth, then this mass is significant. It is this force that causes objects to accelerate towards the Earth at 9.81 m/s^2 when they are "free falling".

Newton's Three Laws of Motion

Newton's three laws of motion allow us a set of rules to use when dealing with forces.

PHYSICS GRADE 12

Newton's First Law: An object at rest will remain at rest, or if it is in a **constant** state of motion it will remain in that state unless acted upon by an **unbalanced** external force.

This law tells us that if an object has a **constant** velocity in a straight line then *all* forces acting on it must be balanced. That is, there is no **net** force.

BALANCED   **UNBALANCED**
                                The net force is 5 N to the right.

Newton's Second Law: If an unbalanced force acts on an object, then the object will **accelerate** in the direction of the **net** force.

Mathematically, this is written

$$F = ma$$

but $F_{net} = ma$ is more correct.

This law tells us that *if an object is accelerating, then there must be an unbalanced force acting on the object.*

Newton's Third Law: For every action force, there is an equal and opposite reaction force.

This law tells us that forces always appear in pairs, but act on different objects. If I push on you with a force of 20 N, then at the same time you are exerting an equal force on me.

PHYSICS GRADE 12

Work

Work is a useful method for determining **energy** used or gained. Since work is defined in physics as being dome whenever a force moves an object a distance in the direction of the force, it is useful to remember.

Work = Force x Distance

$$W = F \times d$$

Sometimes the force does not act in the same direction as the motion. Therefore it is important to determine the amount of force (that component of the force) that acts in the direction of motion.

For example, push a lawnmower

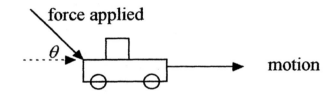

F_x is the force doing work. Therefore

$$F_x = F_A \cos\theta$$

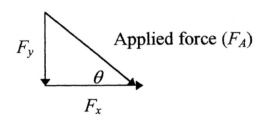

so   Work $= F \cos\theta \, (d)$

$$W = Fd \cos\theta$$

PHYSICS GRADE 12

Circular Motion

An object traveling in a circle at a constant speed is continuously changing its velocity by changing direction. The force required to cause this acceleration is a centipetal force (F_c). This force is always directed towards the centre of the circle. It is often difficult to determine what it is that is supplying this force.

A ball twirled on a string has the centripetal force supplied by the string. If the string were cut, the ball would fly off in a direction tangent to the circle at the point where the string is cut.

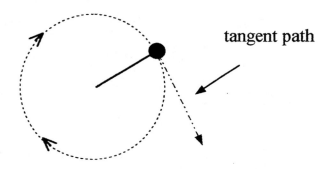

tangent path

The Earth travels in a nearly circular path as it orbits the Sun. The **force of gravity** supplies the necessary centripetal force that maintains this circular motion. It is important to remember that F_c can be determined from

$$F_c = \frac{mv^2}{R}$$

where m = mass of object traveling in circular path

v = speed of object

R = radius of circular path

or, since for an object traveling at a constant speed in a circular path the object must travel a distance equal to the **circumference**, $2\pi R$, in a time T, called the **period of rotation**.

then
$$F_c = \frac{m\left(\dfrac{2\pi R}{T}\right)^2}{R} = \frac{\dfrac{m4\pi^2 R^2}{T^2}}{R} = \frac{m4\pi^2}{T^2}$$

and
$$F_c = \frac{4\pi^2 mR}{T^2}$$

Waves

There are two ways to transfer energy across space

     1- by particles like bullets or basketball, or

     2- by waves.

Waves are classified as two types:

     1- **Mechanical waves** - those that need a medium (some substance) to travel through.

          Water waves need water.
          Sound wave need air, or steel, or etc.

     2 - **Electromagnetic waves** - no need for a medium.

Mechanical waves are classified by the direction of vibration of particles in the medium in relation to the direction of energy propagation.

PHYSICS GRADE 12

a) Transverse Waves (like water waves)

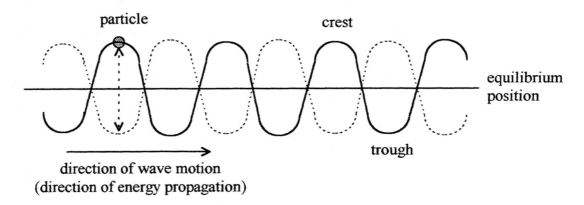

Particles in the medium move perpendicular to this direction.

b) Longitudinal Waves (sound waves)

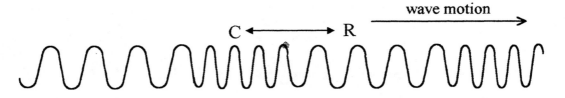

The particles in the medium vibrate parallel to the direction of energy transfer. In longitudinal waves we find regions of varying density. The high density region is called a **compression** (C). A low density region is called a **rarefaction** (R).

   Whether transverse or longitudinal, all waves share certain characteristics.

   1- They are created by vibrating objects. A vibration is a **back and forth** motion. One complete vibration is called a **cycle** and this produces one wave. Many cycles produce a **wave train**. A transverse wave contains one crest and one trough. A longitudinal wave contains one compression and one rarefaction.

2- The time required for one complete vibration is called **the period of vibration** (T). This is the time to produce one wave, and is also **the period** of the wave.

3- Waves, once produced, move through the medium as a disturbance in all directions from the source that created them.

4- The amount of energy carried by the wave depends upon the **amplitude** (a) of the wave. This is a measure of the maximum displacement of a particle in the medium from its normal rest, or **equilibrium** position.

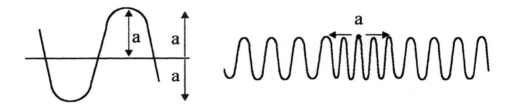

5- The **frequency of vibration** (*f*) creating the waves is the number of complete vibrations per unit of time. Ten complete back and forth motions per second produces waves with a frequency of 10 waves/sec. or 10 cycles/s or 10 Hz. Hz is the symbol for Hertz (waves/second). This abbreviation is used only when the time unit is seconds. The frequency of a wave and its period are inversely related. That is

$$f = \frac{1}{T} \quad \text{or} \quad T = \frac{1}{f}$$

6- Every wave has a **wavelength** (λ). This is the distance from a point on one wave to the corresponding point on the next wave

---

in a wave train. Both points must have the same velocity and displacement to correspond. Often wavelength is measured from crest to crest in a transverse wave, or from compression to compression in a longitudinal wave.

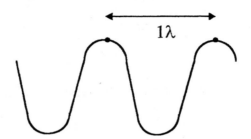

7- Every wave has a velocity. Since $v = \dfrac{d}{t}$, and d is measured

in λ's, and t by T for a wave, then

$$v = \frac{\lambda}{T} \quad \text{but} \quad T = \frac{1}{f} \quad \text{so}$$

$$v = \frac{\lambda}{\frac{1}{f}} = \lambda f.$$

$$\boxed{v = \lambda f}$$

This is the **universal wave equation**.

The speed of a mechanical wave is determined by the medium through which the wave moves. In other words, sound waves travel through air at about 330 m/s. This speed cannot be changed until the wave changes mediums. The frequency of the waves depends on the frequency of the source. The frequency can only be changed at the source. If a tuning fork vibrates at

can only be changed at the source. If a tuning fork vibrates at 125 Hz, it produces sound waves that travel through air at 330 m/s. These waves will have a λ given by

$$\lambda = \frac{v}{f} = \frac{330 \text{ m/s}}{125 \text{ waves/s}} = 2.64 \text{ m/wave}$$

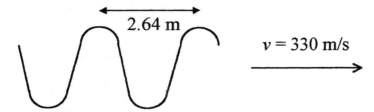

If the frequency is increased to 500 Hz, then the waves still travel at 330 m/s, but the λ is decreased to 0.66 m.

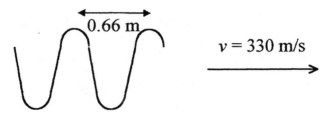

Since v is constant, $\lambda \propto \frac{1}{f}$. As f increases, λ decreases.

8- All waves exhibit wave behavior and certain properties.

a) **reflection**- All waves reflect (more in light unit)

b) **refraction**- this is the change of direction that occurs when a wave changes mediums.

c) **diffraction**- this is the spreading through openings, or bending around corners characteristic of waves

d) **interference**- two different waves traveling through the same medium can join *constructively* (build a larger wave) or *destructively* (cancel each other out).

PHYSICS GRADE 12

Light

The Sun is our main supplier of energy to the Earth. This energy, stored by green plants, is transported across millions of kilometers of space by visible light. What is the *nature* of light ? Does it carry its energy by particles, or by waves ? This question was debated for many centuries. Over the last number of centuries, many discoveries were made about light- its properties and characteristics. Some information supports a particle model for light, other information supports a wave model. We know:

1- *light is emitted* from sources like burning wood, incandescent light bulbs, fluorescent lights, burning oil or gas, glowing hot steel, fireflies, etc. Light never appears mysteriously from nowhere, but always has its origin from some matter.

2- once produced, it travels trough vacant space at an incredibly fast rate. i.e. 299, 792, 456.5 m/s $\pm$ 1 m/s. This value is constant, and is given the value **c= 3.00 x 10^8 m/s**.

3- when it strikes a surface, depending on the properties of the material, the energy carried by the light will always be partially absorbed, partially reflected, and possibly even partially transmitted through the material.

4- *light needs no medium* and can travel trough free space.

5- *light travels in straight lines*. In light diagrams, we can think of light as being transmitted through space as waves or particles.

PHYSICS GRADE 12

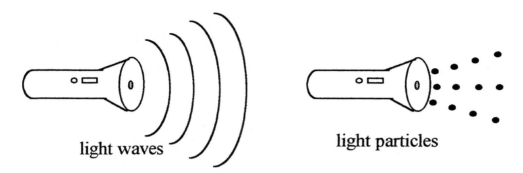

light waves

light particles

To simplify light diagrams, we use **rays**
to indicate the direction of light propagation.

light rays

Since a point light source will cause shadows with sharp edges, we know
that light travels in straight lines.

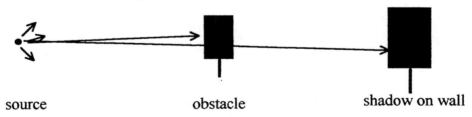

source   obstacle   shadow on wall

A meter stick casts a shadow 1.35 m long. How long would the shadow of
a 4.5 m pole be at the same time of day ?

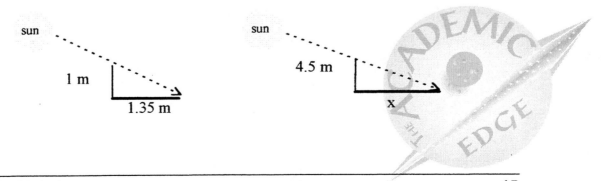

sun

1 m

1.35 m

sun

4.5 m

x

6- *Light reflects:*

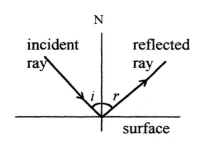

In reflection diagrams, a line called a normal line is drawn at the point where an incident ray reflects from the surface of an object. The normal is always drawn perpendicular to the surface. Then, the **law of reflection** tells us that

$$< i = < r$$

7- *light refracts:*

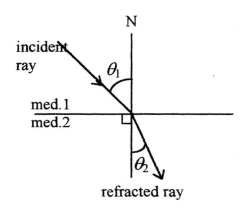

refracted ray

Refraction refers to the change in direction that occurs when a wave (light) passes from one medium (like air) into a second medium (like water) **obliquely**. Obliquely means that the incident ray is not perpendicular to the boundary separating the two mediums.

The angle of incidence and the angle of refraction are always measured from the incident ray to the normal, and from the refracted ray to the normal. Since refraction occurs because of different speeds for the wave in each medium, then light will travel at v_1 in medium #1, and at v_2 in medium #2. Then θ_1 and θ_2 are related to v_1 and v_2 as

$$\frac{\sin\theta_1}{\sin\theta_2} = \frac{v_1}{v_2}$$

Since the frequency of a wave can only be changed at the source creating the wave, then the frequency remains equal in medium 1 and medium 2.

since $v_1 = f_1 \lambda_1$ and $v_2 = f_2 \lambda_2$

the above relationship can be expressed using wavelengths.

$$\frac{\sin\theta_1}{\sin\theta_2} = \frac{v_1}{v_2} = \frac{\lambda_1}{\lambda_2}$$

Now, if a material is transparent, light can then pass through it, but the speed of the light in the medium is always less that the speed of light in a vacuum. The **index of refraction**, n, tells us the ratio of

$$n = \frac{\text{speed of light in vacuum}}{\text{speed of light in medium}} \quad \text{or} \quad n = \frac{c}{v},$$

where v is the speed of light in the medium where the index of refraction is being determined.

n = 1   for air or a vacuum   (light has highest speed)

n = 1.33   for water

n = 1.6   for glass

n = 2.4   for diamonds   (light has slowest speed)

The greater value of n tells me that the speed of light in that medium is slower. We often refer to the index of refraction as being a measure of **optical density**. If the density is high, then n is large, and light travels slowly through that medium. If the density is low, then n is close to 1 (minimum value), and the light will travel at close to 3.00×10^8 m/s through that medium (highest possible speed). A general rule for working with refraction is this:

PHYSICS GRADE 12

If light moves from a medium of low density to one of high density, the refracted ray is bent *towards* the normal.

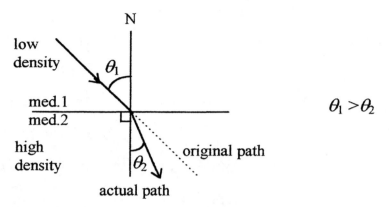

$\theta_1 > \theta_2$

but if it goes from a region of high density to low density, then the refracted ray is bent *away* from the normal.

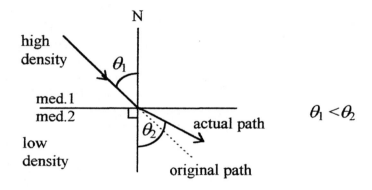

$\theta_1 < \theta_2$

The **law of refraction** in its complete form is:

$$\frac{\sin\theta_1}{\sin\theta_2} = \frac{v_1}{v_2} = \frac{\lambda_1}{\lambda_2} = \frac{n_2}{n_1}$$

8- *light diffracts*, but because it has such a short wavelength, it is not noticeable under normal conditions. To observe diffraction for light, the light must be passed through openings with a size of 10^{-7} m, but when light does this, a noticeable diffraction pattern is produced - *wave model support*.

PHYSICS GRADE 12

9- *light interference*:

If light is passed through two slits, diffraction will occur at each slit and an interference pattern can be observed on a screen a distance from the slits. The interference pattern is a series of bright and dark lines.

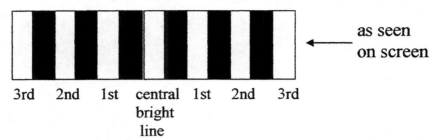

3rd   2nd   1st   central   1st   2nd   3rd
                  bright
                  line

On each side of the **central bright line** (often called the central maximum) are other bright lines, or maxima, called 1st order bright lines, 2nd order bright lines, etc. In a diagram, where S_1 and S_2 are the slits

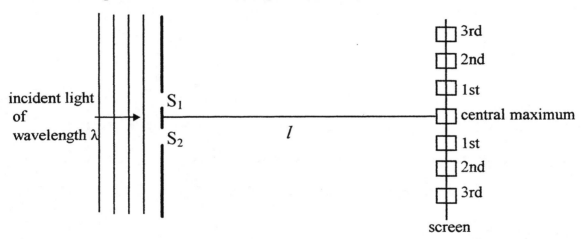

It is possible to determine the λ of the incident wave (light or otherwise).

If   d = distance between the slits (measured from their centres)

            l = distance from slits to screen

            x = distance between any two bright lines

are known, then $\lambda = \dfrac{dx}{nl}$,   where n = 1, 2, 3,...

If x is the distance from central bright line to a 1st order bright line on either side, then n = 1.

If x is the distance from central bright line to a 2nd order bright line on either side, then n =2.

If x is the distance from central bright line to a 3rd order bright line on either side, then n =3, and so on.

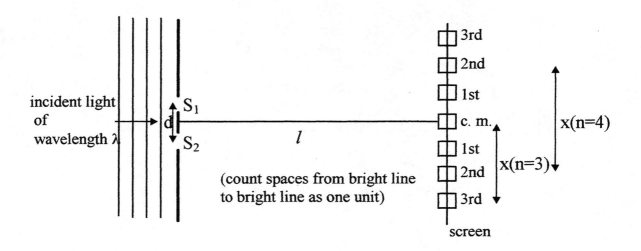

Often a **diffraction grating** is used to obtain an interference pattern. Such a grating is rules with thin lines. The spaces between the lines act like the two slits in the double-slit apparatus described above. If it is ruled at 5000 lines/cm, then $d = \dfrac{1}{5000}\dfrac{cm}{line}$.

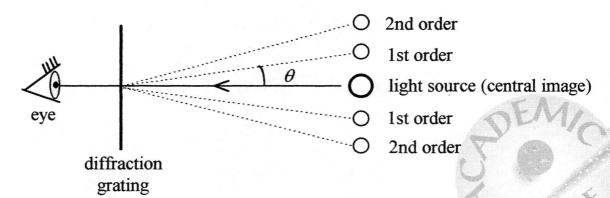

$$\lambda = \frac{d \sin\theta}{n}$$

where $n = 1$ for 1st order image

            $n = 2$ for 2nd order image

and $\theta =$ the angle measured from the central line to the line connecting the image from centre of the diffraction grating.

Interference provides support for the wave model for light. The bright lines are the *ends* of **antinodal** lines (line in the interference pattern) along which **constructive interference** is occurring. The dark spaces in between are the ends of **nodal** lines.

10- *light can be scattered* by small particles. If you've been to a dance, you may have seen coloured light scattered by a fog machine. For light, the amount of scattering depends upon the wavelength of the light. Shorter wavelengths are scattered more than long. It is scattering of blue light in our atmosphere by small particles that gives our sky its blue colour.

11- *Polarization*: Transverse waves can be polarized (that is, their up and down vibrating motion is in one plane only). Unpolarized light has vibrations in many planes, but after passing through a polarizing filter, all vibrations are canceled (or absorbed by the filter) except for one plane.

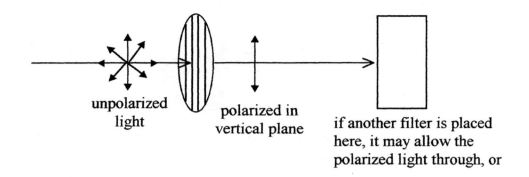

unpolarized light

polarized in vertical plane

if another filter is placed here, it may allow the polarized light through, or

Polarizing filters often show an axis of polarization.

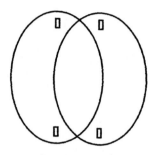

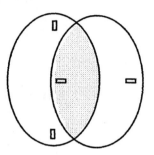

Light can easily pass through both filters, as axis are parallel.

Light is blocked. Axis are perpendicular to each other. Light is canceled

The human eye cannot determine if light is polarized or not, but a single polarizing filter will appear darker, and then lighter when that light is passed through the filter at the same time as the filter is rotated. Polarization can only be explained using a wave model for light. It can only be explained using transverse wave theory. Therefore, it is believed that **light** is a **transverse wave**.

Because physics 30 examines electromagnetic radiation, then you should already be familiar with these ideas about visible light from physics 20. Since visible light is electromagnetic radiation, you need only to extend these ideas to the other ranges of EM radiation to predict the behavior of radio waves, infrared waves, ultraviolet, x-rays, etc.

For example: If blue light is scattered more than red, then ultraviolet should be scattered even more than blue, while infrared should be scattered less than red!

Note: Light has many other properties and behaviors that we could not begin to fully describe in the confines of this note book. The above information is designed to familiarize you with the *main* properties and behaviors of light - those I feel are most important for your understanding of physics 30 concepts. It is suggested that you spend some time researching light.

PHYSICS GRADE 12

Conservation Laws

This unit is concerned with showing that when matter interacts certain quantities remain the same before the interaction as after the interaction. It gives us a belief in the continuity of our universe and allows us to solve problems concerning mass, energy, and momentum.

1) Law of Conservation of Mass

"In any chemical reaction, the mass of the reactants equals the mass of the products."

If 8 g of oxygen gas reacts with 1 g of hydrogen gas, then it is always expected that 9 g of water will result.

$$\text{reactants} \qquad \text{products}$$
$$8\,g + 1\,g \;=\; 9\,g$$

2) Law of Conservation of Energy

"Energy cannot be created nor destroyed, but it may undergo a change in its form."

Energy is that hard to understand quantity that is defined simply as "the ability to do work". Simply, this means that if an object has energy, then it has the ability to do work. **Work** is used in physics to measure energy changes. Therefore, by definition, work (W) is done whenever a force (F) acts on an object and moves it a distance (d), or

$$\boxed{W = F\,d}$$

When work is done on an object, then that object has energy. An object has what is called **mechanical energy**.

PHYSICS GRADE 12

The mechanical energy of an object is simply the sum of its potential energy (stored energy) and kinetic energy (energy of its motion).

$$E = PE + KE$$

The potential energy of an object depends upon its position, or condition. An object is raised above the Earth by exerting a force upwards (against the force of gravity). Because the force acts over a distance (height), work was done on the object A. The object now has Potential Energy (PE) equal to work that was done on it, or

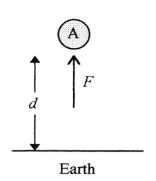

$$PE = W$$

$$PE = F d$$

The force must equal the downward weight of the object, so since

weight $= mg$ where $m = $ mass
$g = $ acceleration due to gravity

and $F = mg$

then

$$PE = mgd$$

Since $d = $ height $= h$, then $PE = mgh$

The PE of an object described like this is called **the gravitational potential energy** of the object. It is believed that object A is on the Earth, this PE = 0, since $h = 0$. There are many other forms of potential energy. A compressed spring has 'elastic potential energy'. A pair of magnets separated by a distance has 'magnetic potential energy'. Gasoline has 'chemical potential energy'.

Now object A with a gravitational potential energy = *mgh* has the ability to do work. If it is released it will fall down, and will be able to exert a force on any object it lands on. As object A falls, its PE is converted into **kinetic energy**. This is the energy that an object has because of its motion.

The kinetic energy of an object is given by

$$KE = \frac{1}{2}mv^2, \quad \text{where} \qquad m = \text{mass of object}$$
$$v = \text{speed of object}$$

If air resistance (or friction) is neglected, then the PE is completely converted into KE by the time the object reaches the Earth. When object A strikes the Earth, the KE is converted into thermal energy (heat).

If the Earth and the object are considered to *be an isolated system of objects*, the law of conservation of energy can be restated as

"In an isolated frictionless system, the total mechanical energy remains constant"

For example,

E=100 J (A)   Total Energy = PE as KE = 0   *100 J of PE*

E=100 J (A)   As object A falls   *say 40 J of PE have*
                Total Energy = PE+KE   *been converted into 40*
                                           J of KE, then
                                           E = KE+PE
                                           = 40 J + 60 J
                                           = 100 J

E=100 J (A)   Total Energy = KE as PE=0   *100 J of KE*
_____
Earth

PHYSICS GRADE 12

A pendulum is a conservative system.

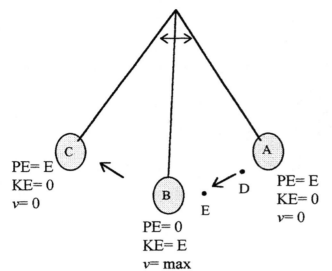

A pendulum constantly converts PE to KE to PE to KE to PE etc. At any given moment, the *total* mechanical energy is a constant.

PE at highest point = KE at lowest point.

or $\quad$ $PE_{highest\ point} = KE_{lowest\ point} = PE + KE$ at *any* point.

Energy at A or C = Energy at B = Energy at D or E

3) Law of Conservation of Momentum

Momentum is a measure of the *quantity of motion* an object has. It is given by

$$p = mv, \quad \text{where} \qquad p = \text{momentum}$$
$$v = \text{velocity}$$
$$m = \text{mass}$$

p is a vector quantity. When an unbalanced force acts on an object, it causes the object to accelerate.

$$F_{net} = ma, \quad \text{but} \quad a = \frac{\Delta v}{t}$$

so $\qquad F = \frac{m\Delta v}{t}$

by rearrangement $Ft = m\Delta v$

The right hand side is simply a *change in momentum* (Δp),

or $\Delta p = m \, \Delta v$

The left hand side tells us that when a net force acts on a mass for a time t, it will cause the object to change its momentum by changing its velocity.

Ft is called an **impulse**.

Newton's third law of motion tells us for every action force there is an equal and opposite reaction force. That is, if a bat exerts a force on a ball, then the ball exerts an equal force on the bat. The two objects experience equal forces, but in opposite direction.

F_1 , direction of force of bat on ball

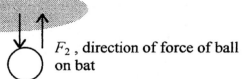

Now, $F_1 = -F_2$.

F_2 , direction of force of ball on bat

The forces act on each object for the same period of time, therefore

$$F_1 \, t = -F_2 \, t$$

but $F_1 \, t = \Delta p$ for ball

and $-F_2 \, t = \Delta p$ for bat

which tells us that if the ball is to gain some momentum in the interaction, then the bat must lose that momentum. To restate the **Law of Conservation of momentum**, "In an isolated system, the total momentum remains constant, regardless of what happens in the system." The total momentum of the system is the *vector* sum of the moments of all the bodies in that system. Internal forces, in a system including a bat and a

bodies in that system. Internal forces, in a system including a bat and a ball for instance, cannot change the momentum of the system. It is possible to change the momentum by using net external forces only.

When dealing with momentum, the key idea is to remember that the momentum of the system *before* something happens in that system must be there *after* the event happens. Often, this is shown algebraically as

$$p_{before} = p_{after}$$

PHYSICS GRADE 12

Energy Conservation Law Solved Problems

1. *A 1.5 x 10³ kg mass is dropped 3.0 meters onto a post, and drives the post 0.50 m into the ground.*

a) How much energy does the weight deliver to the post.

Answer: In this question, the energy getting to the post must come from the 1500 kg mass. So if we know how much energy (PE) it had at its highest point, this would be the energy that the mass could deliver to the post. Therefore,

$$PE = mgh$$
$$= 1500 \text{ kg } (9.8 \text{ m/s}^2)(3 \text{ m})$$
$$= 44, 100 \text{ J}$$
$$= 4.4 \text{ x } 10^4 \text{ J}$$

b) How much **work** *can the weight of the mass do ?*

Answer: Since the energy stored by the mass at the height of 3 m means that the mass has the ability to do work, then it can do as much work as it has energy. Therefore,

$$\text{Work available} = 4.4 \text{ x } 10^4 \text{ J.}$$

c) With what average force does it drive the post ?

Answer:

Since work= Fd, then

$$F = \frac{W}{d} = \frac{4.4 \text{ x } 10^4 \text{ J}}{0.50 \text{ m}} = 8.8 \text{ x } 10^4 \text{ N}$$

d) What will the velocity of the mass be just before it strikes the post ?

Answer: Since energy is conserved, we know that the amount of PE at the highest point = the KE at the lowest point. Therefore,

$$PE = KE$$

$$mgh = (mv^2)/2$$

$$2gh = v^2$$

$$v = \sqrt{2gh} = \sqrt{2\left(9.8 \text{ m} / \text{s}^2\right)(3 \text{ m})} = 7.7 \text{ m} / \text{s} \; \textit{downwards.}$$

PHYSICS GRADE 12

Energy Conservation Law Practice Problems

1. A spring is compressed 15 cm by an average force of 75 N.

a) What is the potential energy of the spring ?

b) If the spring is used to shoot a pebble with a mass of 10 g, how high will the pebble rise ?

c) At what velocity will the pebble leave the spring ?

2. What is the kinetic energy of a 4.0 kg rock that has fallen 5.0 m ?

3. A 10 kg object is raised 20 m and then dropped. After it has fallen 8.0 m, find

a) its kinetic energy

b) its potential energy

c) Is the sum of a) + b) equal to the PE of the object when it was 20 m high ?

4. A 50 g rock is dropped from a bridge that is 350 m above water.

a) What is the KE of the rock as it hits the water ?

b) What is its velocity when it strikes the water ?

5. A ball with a mass of 250 g is caught by a ball player, and is stopped in a distance of 0.50 m. The ball player was traveling at 24 m/s when it struck his hand.

a) What was the ball's KE ?

b) How much work did it do on the hand of the ballplayer ?

c) What becomes of the energy of the ball ?

d) with what average force did it strike the hand ?

6. a) How much work must be done on a 0.8 kg ball to give it a velocity of 36 m/s ?

b) If your hand moves 1.2 m while throwing the ball, what is the average force that you apply ?

7. A pendulum is raised 0.60 m above its point of lowest descent. When it is released, what will its velocity be after it has dropped to its lowest point of travel ?

8. A 45 kg bungee jumper falls 25 m. At this point, the rubber leg strap starts to slow the jumper down. The jumper falls a further 5 m before stopping.

a) What was the PE of the jumper before he jumped ?

b) What we the KE of the jumper when the rubber leg strap took effect ?

c) What was the average force exerted by the strap to slow the bungee jumper down ?

d) How much work did the rubber strap do ?

PHYSICS GRADE 12

9. A clock is wound by raising a 4 kg mass 5.0 m. The clock will run for 30 hours on one such winding.

a) How much PE is stored in the clock's winding mechanism ?

b) What is the power consumption of the clock ?
(Remember ! Power = Energy/Time)

10. A 75.0 kg skydiver (with a bad parachute) falls 1500 m. and sinks 1.5 m into the water of a lake before stopping. What was the average force of the impact ?

PHYSICS GRADE 12

Energy Conservation Law Practice Problem Solutions

1. A spring is compressed 15 cm by an average force of 75 N.
a) What is the potential energy of the spring ?

Answer: Since   W = PE when compressed, since it is not moving,

and $W = Fd$

$$PE = Fd = (75 \text{ N})(0.15 \text{ m}) = \textbf{11 J}$$

b) If the spring is used to shoot a pebble with a mass of 10 g, how high will the pebble rise ?

Answer: At the highest point, the pebble is stopped, so all the

compressional PE_c is transformed into gravitational PE_g.

so $PE_c = PE_g = 11$ J

$PE_g = mgh$

therefore $h = \dfrac{PE_g}{mg} = \dfrac{11 \text{ J}}{(0.01 \text{ kg})(9.8 \text{ m/s}^2)} = \textbf{1.2 x 10}^2 \textbf{ m}$

c) At what velocity will the pebble leave the spring ?

Answer: As the pebble leaves the spring, all the compressional PE is

tranformed into KE,

so $KE = \dfrac{1}{2}mv^2$ and $v^2 = \dfrac{2KE}{m}$

therefore $v = \sqrt{\dfrac{2KE}{m}} = \sqrt{\dfrac{2(11 \text{ J})}{0.01 \text{ kg}}} = \textbf{47 m/s}$

---

2. What is the kinetic energy of a 4.0 kg rock that has fallen 5.0 m ?

Answer: The rock only had PE before being dropped, so

$$PE = mgh = (4.0 \text{ kg})(9.8 \text{ m/s}^2)(5.0 \text{ m})$$
$$= 2.0 \times 10^2 \text{ J}$$

After falling, all this PE is transformed into KE,

therefore KE = **2.0 x 10² J**

3. A 10 kg object is raised 20 m and then dropped. After it has fallen 8.0 m, find

a) its kinetic energy

Answer: We can find the KE if we find its velocity after falling 8.0 m.

$$\text{Since} \quad v_{8\,m}^2 - v_{20\,m}^2 = 2ad$$
$$v_{8\,m}^2 = v_{20\,m}^2 + 2ad = 0 \text{ m}^2/\text{s}^2 + 2(9.8 \text{ m/s}^2)(8.0 \text{ m})$$
$$= 1.6 \times 10^2 \text{ m}^2/\text{s}^2$$

$$\text{and} \quad KE = \frac{1}{2}mv^2 = \frac{1}{2}(10 \text{ kg})(1.6 \times 10^2 \text{ m}^2/\text{s}^2)$$
$$= \mathbf{7.8 \times 10^2 \text{ J}}$$

b) its potential energy

Answer: After falling a distance of 8.0 m, it is 20 m - 8.0 m = 12 m
above   the ground, so

$$PE = mgh = (10 \text{ kg})(9.8 \text{ m/s}^2)(12 \text{ m})$$
$$= \mathbf{1.2 \times 10^3 \text{ J}}$$

c) Is the sum of a) + b) equal to the PE of the object when it was 20 m high ?

Answer: At 20 m: $PE = mgh = (10 \text{ kg})(9.8 \text{ m/s}^2)(20 \text{ m})$

$$= 2.0 \text{ x } 10^3 \text{ J}$$

Adding the answers from a) and b):

$$7.9 \text{ x } 10^2 \text{ J} + 1.2 \text{ x } 10^3 \text{ J}$$

$$= 7.9 \text{ x } 10^2 \text{ J} + 12 \text{ x } 10^2 \text{ J (need same exponent)}$$

$$= 20 \text{ x } 10^2 \text{ J} = 2.0 \text{ x } 10^3 \text{ J}$$

they are the same.

4. A 50 g rock is dropped from a bridge that is 350 m above water.
a) What is the KE of the rock as it hits the water ?

Answer: Note that $50g = 50g \text{ x } \dfrac{1 \text{ kg}}{1000g} = 0.050 \text{ kg.}$

Before the rock is released, it only has PE

so $\qquad PE = mgh = (0.050 \text{ kg})(9.8 \text{ m/s}^2)(350 \text{ m})$

$$= 1.7 \text{ x } 10^2 \text{ J}$$

As it hits the water, all the PE is transformed into KE,

so $\qquad KE = 1.7 \text{ x } 10^2 \text{ J}$

b) What is its velocity when it strikes the water ?

Answer: $KE = \dfrac{1}{2}mv^2$ and $v^2 = \dfrac{2KE}{m}$

therefore $v = \sqrt{\dfrac{2KE}{m}} = \sqrt{\dfrac{2(1.7 \text{ x } 10^2 \text{ J})}{0.05 \text{ kg}}} = \textbf{83 m/s}$

5. A ball with a mass of 250 g is caught by a ball player, and is stopped in a distance of 0.50 m. The ball player was traveling at 24 m/s when it struck his hand.

a) What was the ball's KE ?

Answer: Note that $250g = 250g \times \dfrac{1 \text{ kg}}{1000g} = 0.250 \text{ kg.}$

$$KE = \frac{1}{2}mv^2 = \frac{1}{2}(0.250 \text{ kg})(24 \text{ m/s})^2 = \mathbf{72 \ J}$$

b) How much work did it do on the hand of the ballplayer ?

Answer: $\qquad$ $W = KE = \mathbf{72 \ J}$

c) What becomes of the energy of the ball ?

Answer: It is transformed into heat, sound, and deformation of the glove.

d) with what average force did it strike the hand ?

Answer: $\qquad$ $F = \dfrac{W}{d} = \dfrac{72 \text{ J}}{0.50 \text{ m}} = \mathbf{144 \ N}$

6. a) *How much work must be done on a 0.8 kg ball to give it a velocity of 36 m/s ?*

Answer: The work done is equal to the kinetic energy given to the ball,

$$W = KE$$

so $W = \frac{1}{2}mv^2 = \frac{1}{2}(0.8\ kg)(36\ m/s)^2 = \mathbf{5\ x\ 10^2\ J}$

b) *If your hand moves 1.2 m while throwing the ball, what is the average force that you apply ?*

Answer: $F = \frac{W}{d} = \frac{5\ x\ 10^2\ J}{1.2\ m} = \mathbf{4\ x\ 10^2\ N}$

7. *A pendulum is raised 0.60 m above its point of lowest descent. When it is released, what will its velocity be after it has dropped to its lowest point of travel ?*

Answer: When it is raised 0.60 m, it has PE

$$PE = mgh = m(9.8\ m/s^2)(0.60\ m) = m\ x\ 5.9\ m^2/s^2$$

At the lowest point, all this PE is tranformed into KE, so

$$PE = KE$$

$$m\ x\ 5.9\ m^2/s^2 = \frac{1}{2}mv^2$$

so $v^2 = 2(5.9\ m^2/s^2) = 11.8\ m^2/s^2$

and $v = \mathbf{3.4\ m/s}$

---

8. *A 45 kg bungee jumper falls 25 m. At this point, the rubber leg strap starts to slow the jumper down. The jumper falls a further 5 m before stopping.*
a) What was the PE of the jumper before he jumped ?

Answer: The potential energy, relative to the point where the strap begind to stretch is,

$$PE = mgh = (45 \text{ kg})(9.8 \text{ m/s}^2)(25 \text{ m})$$
$$= \textbf{1.1 x 10}^4 \textbf{ J}$$

b) What we the KE of the jumper when the rubber leg strap took effect ?

Answer: The potential energy before he jumped equals the KE when the strap takes effect.

$$KE = PE = \textbf{1.1 x 10}^4 \textbf{ J}$$

c) What was the average force exerted by the strap to slow the bungee jumper down ?

Answer: Since W to stop the jumper = KE = 1.1 x 10^4 J

$$F = \frac{W}{d} = \frac{1.1 \times 10^4 \text{ J}}{5.0 \text{ m}} = \textbf{2.2 x 10}^3 \textbf{ N}$$

d) How much work did the rubber strap do ?

Answer: Work to stop the jumper = KE = **1.1 x 10^4 J**

9. *A clock is wound by raising a 4 kg mass 5.0 m. The clock will run for 30 hours on one such winding.*
a) How much PE is stored in the clock's winding mechanism ?

Answer: The potential energy stored comes is equal to the PE of the

raised   mass.

so $PE = mgh = (4.0 \text{ kg})(9.8 \text{ m/s}^2)(5.0 \text{ m})$

$$= \textbf{2.0 x 10}^2 \textbf{ J}$$

b) What is the power consumption of the clock ?
(Remember ! Power = Energy/Time)

Answer: We need to know time in seconds:

$$30 \text{ hrs x } \frac{60 \text{ min}}{1 \text{ hr}} \text{ x} \frac{60 \text{ s}}{1 \text{ min}} = 1.08 \times 10^5 \text{ s}$$

$$P = \frac{E}{t} = \frac{2.0 \times 10^2 \text{ J}}{1.08 \times 10^5 \text{ s}} = \textbf{1.8 x 10}^{-3} \textbf{ Watts}$$

10. *A 75.0 kg skydiver (with a bad parachute) falls 1500 m. and sinks 1.5 m into the water of a lake before stopping. What was the average force of the impact ?*

Answer: PE before jumping is

$$PE = mgh = (75.0 \text{ kg})(9.8 \text{ m/s}^2)(1500 \text{ m})$$

$$= \textbf{1.10 x 10}^6 \textbf{ J}$$

Therefore, the force of the impact is:

$$F = \frac{W}{d} = \frac{1.10 \times 10^6 \text{ J}}{1.5 \text{ m}} = \textbf{7.4 x 10}^5 \textbf{ N}$$

PHYSICS GRADE 12

Momentum Conservation Law Solved Problems

1. Determine the momentum of a 50 kg girl running at 5.0 m/s.

Answer: $p=mv = 50$ kg $(5.0$ m/s$)$

$= 250$ kg m/s

2. A 1400 kg car strikes a fence at 10 m/s and came to a stop in 0.8 s. What average force acted on the car ?

Answer: The car had momentum before striking the fence, but none after stopping. The fence must have exerted an external force on the car causing it to change its momentum. Such a force is an **impulse**. Therefore,

$$Ft = \Delta p$$

$$= m \, \Delta v \qquad\qquad \text{but } \Delta v = v_f - v_i$$

$$= m \, (v_f - v_i)$$

$$F = \frac{m(v_f - v_i)}{t}$$

$$= \frac{1400 \text{ kg } (0 \text{ m/s} - 10 \text{ m/s})}{0.8 \text{ s}}$$

$$= \frac{1400 \text{ kg } (-10 \text{ m/s})}{0.8 \text{ s}}$$

$$= -17,500 \text{ N}$$

The negative sign indicates that the force acted in the opposite direction to the initial velocity.

---

3. *A 1200 kg car moving North at 25 m/s collides with a 1600 kg car moving west at 20 m/s. If the cars stick together after the collision, at what velocity and in what direction does the wreckage begin to move ?*

Answer: Sketch diagram.

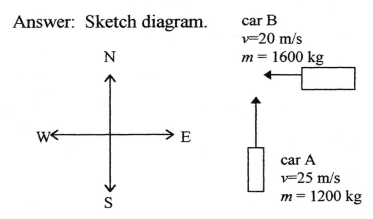

car B
$v = 20$ m/s
$m = 1600$ kg

car A
$v = 25$ m/s
$m = 1200$ kg

We must determine the momentum of the system before the impact. The momentum after must be equal.

$$p_{before} = p_{after}$$

use vector diagram to determine p_{before}.

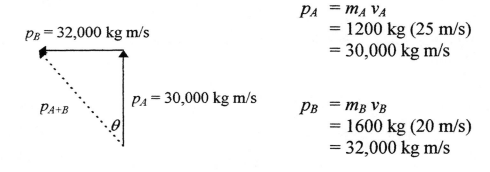

$p_B = 32,000$ kg m/s

$p_A = 30,000$ kg m/s

p_{A+B}

θ

$$p_A = m_A v_A$$
$$= 1200 \text{ kg } (25 \text{ m/s})$$
$$= 30,000 \text{ kg m/s}$$

$$p_B = m_B v_B$$
$$= 1600 \text{ kg } (20 \text{ m/s})$$
$$= 32,000 \text{ kg m/s}$$

$$p_{A+B} = \sqrt{\left(30,000 \text{ kg m / s}\right)^2 + \left(32,000 \text{ kg m / s}\right)^2}$$

using Pythagoreus

$$= 43,863 \text{ kg m/s}$$

$$= 4.4 \times 10^4 \text{ kg m/s} = \text{momentum before the collision (the}$$

vector sum of all bodies)

The direction can be found by using

$$\tan \theta = \frac{32000}{30000}, \text{ so } \theta = 46.8° \text{ counter-clockwise from North.}$$

Now the speed can be determined since the momentum after the collision must be 4.4×10^4 kg m/s.

since $\quad p_{after} = m_A \, v_A{}' + m_B \, v_B{}' \quad \leftarrow$ the ´ means 'after'

$$= (m_A + m_B) \, v' \quad \longleftarrow \text{ they stick together}$$

$$4.4 \times 10^4 \text{ kg m/s} = (1200 \text{ kg} + 1600 \text{ kg}) \, v'$$

$$v' = \frac{4.4 \times 10^4 \text{ kg m/s}}{2800 \text{ kg}}$$

$$= \frac{4.4 \times 10^4 \text{ kg m/s}}{0.28 \times 10^4 \text{ kg}}$$

$$= 15.7 \text{ m/s at } 46.8° \text{ West of North}$$

4. A 40 g bullet moving at 400 m/s strikes a stationary 2 kg sandbag hanging on a string. If the bullet is embedded in the sandbag,
a) How fast does the sandbag move after the bullet strikes it ?

Answer: $\quad\quad\quad p_{before} = p_{after}$

$$[m_{bullet} \, v_{bullet} + m_{bag} \, v_{bag}] = [m_{bullet} + m_{bag}] v \;\longleftarrow$$

before $\quad\quad\quad\quad$ after $\quad\quad$ common velocity after

$$[(0.040 \text{ kg})(400 \text{ m/s}) + 0] = [0.040 \text{ kg} + 2 \text{ kg}] v$$

$$v = \frac{0.040 \text{ kg} (400 \text{ m/s})}{2.040 \text{ kg}} = 7.8 \text{ m/s}$$

b) How high will the bag swing ?

Answer: By conservation of energy, the KE of the bag = PE at its highest point. Therefore,

$$KE = PE$$

$$(mv^2)/2 = mgh$$

$$h = \frac{v^2}{2g} = \frac{(7.8 \text{ m} / \text{s})^2}{2(9.8 \text{ m} / \text{s}^2)} = 3.1 \text{ m}$$

*5. A 2000 kg canon fires a 48 kg shell at 360 m/s. What is the **recoil** velocity of the canon upon firing ?*

Answer: By the conservation of energy, the momentum before the cannon is fired must be equal to the momentum after it is fired as the forces on the he canon and the shell are internal forces.

$$p_{before} = p_{after}$$

but $p_{before} = 0$, cannon and shell not moving. So

$$p_{after} = 0 = p_{shell} + p_{cannon}$$

$$0 = m_{shell} \; v_{shell} + m_{cannon} \; v_{cannon}$$

$$0 = (48 \text{ kg})(360 \text{ m/s}) + (2000 \text{ kg}) \, v'_{cannon}$$

$$-(48 \text{ kg})(360 \text{ m/s}) = (2000 \text{ kg}) \, v'_{cannon}$$

$$v'_c = \frac{-(48 \text{ kg})(360 \text{ m} / \text{s})}{2000 \text{ kg}} = -8.64 \text{ m} / \text{s}$$

The negative sign means that the velocity of the cannon is in the opposite direction to the velocity of the shell.

PHYSICS GRADE 12

Momentum Conservation Law Practice Problems

1. A 2500 kg truck crashes into a wall at 40 km/h, and comes to a stop in 0.8 s. What is the average force on the truck ?

2. A 4 kg and 5 kg rifle fire identical bullets of mass 0.020 kg with a muzzle velocity of 520 m/s. Compare the recoil momenta and the recoil velocities of the two rifles.

PHYSICS GRADE 12

3. A 70 kg man steps horizontally from a 300 kg boat onto a dock with a velocity of 4 m/s. At what velocity will the boat move away from the dock ?

4. A run away car of 1200 kg mass rolls down a hill onto a level road at 18 m/s. To stop the car, a 4000 kg truck will be used. It will meet the car in a head-on collision. What should the truck's velocity be so that both vehicles stop after the collision ?

5. A 60 kg boy is rolling on roller-skates at 8.0 m/s when he catches a 0.6 kg ball moving towards him at 30.0 m/s. What is his velocity after catching the ball ?

6. A 1500 kg car traveling at 15 m/s overtakes a 1200 kg car traveling at 12 m/s and collides with it.

a) If both cars stick together, what is their final velocity ?

b) How much KE is lost ?

c) What % of the original KE is this ?

7. A 1 kg stone moving at 3 m/s south collides with a 5.0 kg mudball moving east at 1.4 m/s, and becomes embedded in the mudball. Determine the velocity (magnitude and direction) of both objects after impact.

8. A 0.80 kg ball traveling at 7 m/s collides head on with a 1.00 kg ball moving at -12.0 m/s in the opposite direction. The 0.80 kg ball moves away at -14.0 m/s after the collision. Find the velocity of the 1.00 kg ball after the collision.

9. An 8.0 kg ball is moving at a velocity of 15 m/s. It collides with a stationary ball of equal mass. After the collision, the first ball moves off in a direction 20° to the left of its original path, and the second ball moves off at 70° to the right of the first ball's original path.

a) Use a vector diagram to find the momentum of the first ball and the second ball after the collision.

b) What is the *speed* of each ball after the collision ?

10. Two cars meet at an intersection. Car A has a mass of 1645 kg and was traveling at 60 km/hr at 40° counter-clockwise from North after the collision. Car B, with a mass of 1200 kg was traveling at 30 km/hr at 54° counter-clockwise from North after the collision. If car A had originally been traveling West, and car B originally traveling North, what were their original velocities before the collision ?

PHYSICS GRADE 12

Momentum Conservation Law Practice Problem Solutions

1. A 2500 kg truck crashes into a wall at 40 km/h, and comes to a stop in 0.8 s. What is the average force on the truck ?

Answer: Since force is measured in Newtons (kg m/s^2), then we must first convert 40 km/hr into m/s.

$$\frac{40 \text{ km}}{1 \text{ hr}} \times \frac{1000 \text{ m}}{1 \text{ km}} \times \frac{1 \text{ hr}}{3600 \text{ s}} = 11 \text{ m/s}$$

The truck had a change in velocity (11 m/s to 0 m/s)

$$\Delta v = v_f - v_i = 0 \text{ m/s} - 11 \text{ m/s} = -11 \text{ m/s}$$

The truck had a corresponding change in momentum

$$\Delta p = m \, \Delta v = 2500 \text{ kg} \, (-11 \text{ m/s}) = -27{,}000 \text{ kg m/s}$$

Since this Δp is caused by an **impulse**, then

$$F_{ave} \, t = \Delta p$$

$$F_{ave} = \frac{\Delta p}{t} = \frac{-27{,}500 \text{ kg}}{0.8 \text{ s}}$$

$$= -34{,}375 \text{ N}$$

$$= \textbf{-3.4 x 10}^4 \textbf{ N}$$

PHYSICS GRADE 12

2. *A 4 kg and 5 kg rifle fire identical bullets of mass 0.020 kg with a muzzle velocity of 520 m/s. Compare the recoil momenta and the recoil velocities of the two rifles.*

Answer:

For 4 kg rifle	*For 5 kg rifle*

$$p_{before} = p_{after}$$

$$0 = m_R \ v_R + m_B \ v_B$$

$$-m_R \ v_R = m_B \ v_B$$

$$v_R = -\frac{m_B v_B}{m_R}$$

$$= \frac{(0.020 \text{ kg})(520 \text{ m/s})}{4 \text{ kg}}$$

$$= \mathbf{2.6 \ m/s}$$

$$p_{before} = p_{after}$$

$$0 = m_R \ v_R + m_B \ v_B$$

$$-m_R \ v_R = m_B \ v_B$$

$$v_R = -\frac{m_B v_B}{m_R}$$

$$= \frac{(0.020 \text{ kg})(520 \text{ m/s})}{5 \text{ kg}}$$

$$= \mathbf{2.1 \ m/s}$$

The recoil momenta (- of $m_B \ v_B$) is identical for both rifles, but the recoil velocity is greater for the less massive rifle.

3. *A 70 kg man steps horizontally from a 300 kg boat onto a dock with a velocity of 4 m/s. At what velocity will the boat move away from the dock ?*

Answer: p_{before} the man steps out of the boat = 0, therefore $p_{after} = 0$.

$$p_{after} = 0 = m_{man} \ v_{man} + m_{boat} \ v_{boat}$$

$$= (70 \text{ kg})(4 \text{ m/s}) + (300 \text{ kg}) \ v_{boat}$$

$$- 280 \text{ kg m/s}^2 = (300 \text{ kg}) \ v_{boat}$$

so $\qquad v_{boat} = \textbf{-0.93 m/s}$

The boat moves at 0.93 m/s in the opposite direction to the man.

---

4. A run away car of 1200 kg mass rolls down a hill onto a level road at 18 m/s. To stop the car, a 4000 kg truck will be used. It will meet the car in a head-on collision. What should the truck's velocity be so that both vehicles stop after the collision ?

Answer: The truck's momentum (in the opposite direction to the car's)

should equal the car's momentum in magnitude, so that

$$p_{before} = p_{after} = 0 \text{ (since both stopped afterwards).}$$

Therefore, $p_{car} = m_{car}\, v_{car} = 1200\text{kg } (18 \text{ m/s}) = 21,000 \text{ kg m/s}$

so $p_{truck} = -21,000 \text{ kg m/s} = 4000 \text{ kg } (v_T)$

$$v_T = \frac{-21,600 \text{ kg m/s}}{4000 \text{ kg}} = \textbf{-5.4 m/s}$$

5. A 60 kg boy is rolling on roller-skates at 8.0 m/s when he catches a 0.60 kg ball moving towards him at 30.0 m/s. What is his velocity after catching the ball ?

Answer:

$m = 0.60$ kg
$v = 30.0$ m/s

$m = 60$ kg
$v = 8$ m/s

$p_{before} = m_{ball}\, v_{ball} + m_{boy}\, v_{boy}$

$= (0.60 \text{ kg})(30.0 \text{ m/s}) + (60 \text{ kg}) (\text{-8 m/s})$

$= 18 \text{ kg m/s} + (\text{-480 kg m/s})$ ⎤ opposite direction

$= \text{-462 kg m/s}$

After the collision, there must remain a total momentum = -462 kg m/s.

Therefore, $p_{after} = (m_{ball} + m_{boy})\, v$ ——— common velocity because stuck together

-462 kg m/s $= (0.60 \text{ kg} + 60 \text{ kg})\, v$

so $v = \dfrac{-462 \text{ kg m/s}}{60.6 \text{ kg}} = \textbf{-7.6 m/s}$

The boy and ball move in the original direction of the boy, but much slower than the boy was moving before the impact.

6. *A 1500 kg car traveling at 15 m/s overtakes a 1200 kg car traveling at 12 m/s and collides with it.*
a) If both cars stick together, what is their final velocity ?

Answer: Both cars are traveling in the same direction, therefore v is positive

for both.

$$p_{before} = p_{after}$$

$$m_A \ v_A + m_B \ v_B = (m_A + m_B) \ v \ '$$

therefore
$$v \ ' = \frac{m_A v_A + m_B v_b}{m_A + m_B}$$

$$= \frac{(1500 \ kg)(15 \ m/s) + (1200 \ kg)(12 \ m/s)}{1500 \ kg + 1200 \ kg}$$

$$= \frac{36,900 \ kg \ m/s}{2700 \ kg} = \textbf{13.7 m/s}$$

b) How much KE is lost ?

Answer:
$$KE_{before} = KE_A + KE_B$$
$$= \frac{1}{2} m_A \ v_A{}^2 + \frac{1}{2} m_B \ v_B{}^2$$
$$= \frac{1}{2}(1500 \ kg)(15 \ m/s)^2 + \frac{1}{2}(1200 \ kg)(12 \ m/s)^2$$
$$= 168,750 \ J + 86,400 \ J = 255, 150 \ J$$

$$KE_{after} = \frac{1}{2} m_{A+B} \ v^2 = \frac{1}{2}(2700 \ kg)(13.7 \ m/s)^2 = 253, 381.5 \ J$$

so $\Delta KE = 255,150 \ J - 253, 381.5 \ J = \textbf{1786.5 J is the energy lost}$.

c) What % of the original KE is this ?

Answer: $\% = \dfrac{1768.55}{255,150} \times 100\% = \textbf{0.69\%}$

(less than 1% of the original KE).

7. *A 1 kg stone moving at 3 m/s south collides with a 5.0 kg mudball moving east at 1.4 m/s, and becomes embedded in the mudball. Determine the velocity (magnitude and direction) of both objects after impact.*

Answer:

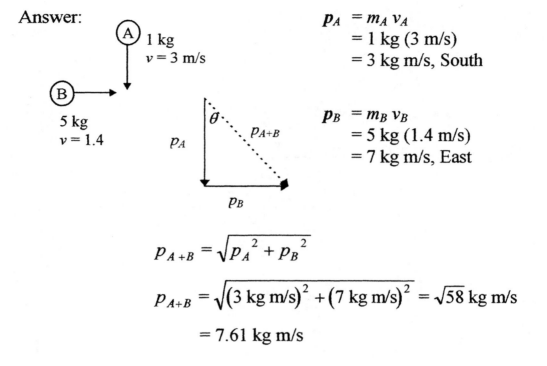

$$p_A = m_A \, v_A$$
$$= 1 \text{ kg (3 m/s)}$$
$$= 3 \text{ kg m/s, South}$$

$$p_B = m_B \, v_B$$
$$= 5 \text{ kg (1.4 m/s)}$$
$$= 7 \text{ kg m/s, East}$$

$$p_{A+B} = \sqrt{p_A{}^2 + p_B{}^2}$$

$$p_{A+B} = \sqrt{(3 \text{ kg m/s})^2 + (7 \text{ kg m/s})^2} = \sqrt{58} \text{ kg m/s}$$

$$= 7.61 \text{ kg m/s}$$

The direction can be found by using

$$\tan \theta = \frac{p_A}{p_B} = \frac{7 \text{ kg m/s}}{3 \text{ kg m/}}, \quad \text{so } \theta = 66.8°$$

Therefore, the mubball and stone move at a velocity that can be determined from their momentum.

Since $\quad p_{A+B} = 7.61 \text{ kg m/s} = m_{A+B} \, v_{A+B}$

$$v_{A+B} = \frac{p_{A+B}}{m_{A+B}} = \frac{7.61 \text{ kg m/s}}{6 \text{ kg}} = \mathbf{1.26 \text{ m/s}}$$

at 66.8° to the East of South, or 336.8° c.c.w. from the positive axis.

8. A 0.80 kg ball traveling at 7 m/s collides head on with a 1.00 kg ball moving at -12.0 m/s in the opposite direction. The 0.80 kg ball moves away at -14.0 m/s after the collision. Find the velocity of the 1.00 kg ball after the collision.

Answer:

$$p_{before} = p_{after}$$

$$m_A \ v_A + m_B \ v_B = m_A \ v_A' + m_B \ v_B'$$

$$(0.80 \text{ kg})(7 \text{ m/s}) + (1 \text{ kg})(-12 \text{ m/s}) = (0.80 \text{ kg})(-14 \text{ m/s}) + (1 \text{ kg})(v_B')$$

$$-6.4 \text{ kg m/s} = -11.2 \text{ kg m/s} + (1 \text{ kg})(v_B')$$

$$-6.4 \text{ kg m/s} + 11.2 \text{ kg m/s} = (1 \text{ kg})(v_B')$$

$$4.8 \text{ kg m/s} = (1 \text{ kg})(v_B')$$

$$\mathbf{4.8 \ m/s} = v_B'$$

The final velocity of the 1.00 kg ball is 4.8 m/s.

9. *An 8.0 kg ball is moving at a velocity of 15 m/s. It collides with a stationary ball of equal mass. After the collision, the first ball moves off in a direction 20° to the left of its original path, and the second ball moves off at 70° to the right of the first ball's original path.*

a) Use a vector diagram to find the momentum of the first ball and the second ball after the collision.

Answer:

Before	*After*

Before

A ·····> B

$m = 8$ kg $\quad m = 8$ kg
$v = 15$ m/s $\quad v = 0$

$p_{before} = m_A \ v_A + m_B \ v_B$

$\qquad = (8 \text{ kg})(15 \text{ m/s}) + 0$

$\qquad = 120 \text{ kg m/s}$

This momentum must remain

after . ⟶
$\qquad\qquad$ 120 kg m/s

After

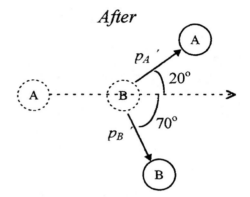

$p_A{}' + p_B{}' = p_{before}$

use vectors

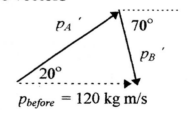

$p_{before} = 120 \text{ kg m/s}$

$p_A{}' = p_{before} (\cos 20°)$

$\qquad = 112.8 \text{ kg m/s at } 20°$

$p_B{}' = p_{before} (\sin 20°)$

$\qquad = 41.0 \text{ kg m/s at } 70°$

b) What is the speed of each ball after the collision ?

Answer: Since $p_A = m_A\, v_A$ then,

$$v_A = \frac{p_A}{m_A} = \frac{112.8 \text{ kg m/s}}{8 \text{ kg}} = \textbf{14.1 m/s}$$

at 20° left of the original path.

and $p_B = m_B\, v_B$

$$v_B = \frac{p_B}{m_B} = \frac{41.0 \text{ kg m/s}}{8 \text{ kg}} = 5.125 \text{ m/s} = \textbf{5.1 m/s}$$

at 70° right of the original path.

10. *Two cars meet at an intersection. Car A has a mass of 1645 kg and was traveling at 60 km/hr at 40° counter-clockwise from North after the collision. Car B, with a mass of 1200 kg was traveling at 30 km/hr at 54° counter-clockwise from North after the collision. If car A had originally been traveling West, and car B originally traveling North, what were their original velocities before the collision ?*

Answer:

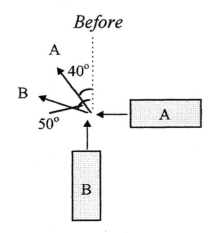

Before

To know the momentums of A and B before the collision, we must determine $p_A + p_B$ after the collision first,

$$p_A \text{ (after)} = m_A\, v_A$$
$$= (1645 \text{ kg})(60 \text{ km/hr})$$
$$= 98700 \text{ kg km/hr at } 40°$$
$$p_B \text{ (after)} = m_B\, v_B$$
$$= (1200 \text{ kg})(30 \text{ km/hr})$$
$$= 36000 \text{ kg km/hr at } 54°$$

Using vectors,

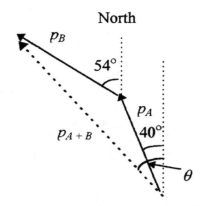

Use the law of cosines to solve for p_{A+B}.

$$(p_{A+B.})^2 = (p_A)^2 + (p_{B.})^2 - 2(p_A)(p_{B.})\cos 166°$$

$$= (98700)^2 + (36000)^2$$

$$- 2(98700)(36000)\cos 166°$$

$$= 1.70 \times 10^{10}$$

$$p_{A+B.} = 1.34 \times 10^5 \text{ kg km/hr}$$

To find angle θ, use law of sines,

$$\frac{p_{A+B}}{\sin 166°} = \frac{p_B}{\sin\theta}$$

$$\frac{134000}{\sin 166°} = \frac{36000}{\sin\theta}$$

$$\sin\theta = \frac{36000(\sin 166°)}{134000}$$

so $\quad \theta = 3.7°$

Therefore, $\quad p_{after}$ is at $40° + 3.7°$ c.c.w. from North.

and $\quad p_{before} = 1.34 \times 10^5$ kg km/hr at $43.7°$ c.c.w. from North.

so $\quad p_A$ (before) $+ p_B$ (before) $= 1.34 \times 10^5$ kg km/hr

Use a vector diagram

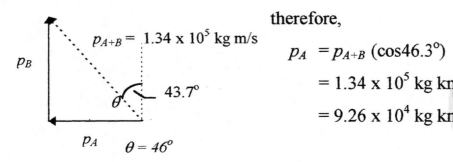

therefore,

$$p_A = p_{A+B} (\cos 46.3°)$$

$$= 1.34 \times 10^5 \text{ kg km/hr } (\cos 46.3°)$$

$$= 9.26 \times 10^4 \text{ kg km/hr}$$

Since $\quad p_A = m_A\, v_A = 9.26 \times 10^4$ kg km/hr

then,

$$v_A = \frac{p_A}{m_A} = \frac{9.26 \times 10^4 \text{ kg km/hr}}{1645 \text{ kg}} = \textbf{56.3 km/hr}$$

East before collision.

and

$$p_B = p_{A+B}\,(\sin 46.3°)$$
$$= 1.34 \times 10^5 \text{ kg km/hr } (\sin 46.3°)$$
$$= 9.69 \times 10^4 \text{ kg km/hr}$$

$$p_B = m_B\, v_B = 9.26 \times 10^4 \text{ kg km/hr}$$

so $\quad v_B = \dfrac{p_B}{m_B} = \dfrac{9.69 \times 10^4 \text{ kg km/ hr}}{1200 \text{ kg}} = \textbf{80.7 km/hr}$

North before collision.

PHYSICS GRADE 12

Electricity and Electric Fields

Electrostatics

When objects are rubbed together, they may become "electrified". For example, rub a balloon on your sweater. When the balloon has been rubbed, it is an electrified object, and it will then attract pieces of lint, grass, paper and other objects. This effect was first discovered in ancient times.

Benjamin Franklin did an exhaustive study of electricity. He was able to show that when an object is electrified or "charged" by rubbing, the forces that act between the charged objects may be forces of **attraction** or **repulsion**. If two identical objects are rubbed with the same material, then the two objects repel, but if they are rubbed with different materials, they may attract each other. Ben Franklin identified two types of electrical charge. He called one '+' and the other '-' (positive and negative).

A positively charged object has a charge that is the same as that acquired by a glass rod when it is rubbed with silk. A negatively charged object has a charge that is the same as that acquired by an ebonite rod (hard rubber) when it is rubbed with fur.

The branch of physics that deals with electrical charges or charged objects and their interactions is called **electrostatics**. The charges are stationary. **Current electricity** deals with charges in motion.

The Laws of Electrostatics state

1- There are two kinds of electric charges, positive and negative.

2- Like charges repel each other, unlike charges attract.

3- If an object is neutral, then it contains equal amounts of + and - charge, and we say it has no **net charge**.

To explain how objects become electrified, we use **atomic theory**.

Atomic Theory

- All objects contain atoms.

- An atom consists of protons, electrons, and neutrons.

- The protons and neutrons are found in the nucleus of the atom.

- Atoms do not change their number of protons or neutrons.

- Each proton in the nucleus carries one positive electrical charge. This is called an elementary positive charge, and is often shown in symbols as $^{+}1e$.

- Neutrons carry no electrical charge, and contribute only to the mass of the atom..

- Electrons are found in each atom outside the nucleus. Each electron carries one negative electrical charge. This is called an elementary negative charge, and is often shown in symbols as $^{-}1e$.

- On the whole, atoms are electrically **neutral**, meaning that in most atoms the number of protons equals the number of electrons. When proton and electrons are together, it seems they cancel each other out if they are in equal numbers.

- Atoms can change their electron count. Electrons can be removed or added to atoms. If an atom *gains* an electron, we say that it is a **negative ion**. If an atom *loses* an electron, we say that it is a **positive ion**.

- We believe that protons are fixed in position in the nucleus and cannot be added or removed, so electrically charged objects owe **their net charge** to the addition or subtraction of electrons.

We can now use atomic theory to explain how an object becomes electrified by rubbing.

When an object is rubbed with another object, electrons will be transferred from one object to the other. The object that *loses* electrons will then acquire a **net + charge**. The other object will gain the electrons and will acquire a **net - charge**. We say a positively charged object has a **deficit** (too few) of electrons. A negatively charged object has **excess** (too many) electrons.

PHYSICS GRADE 12

An electrostatic series can be used to determine the type of net charge an object will acquire.

common substances

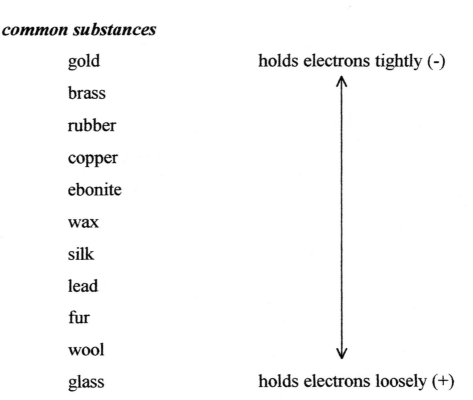

gold	holds electrons tightly (-)
brass	
rubber	
copper	
ebonite	
wax	
silk	
lead	
fur	
wool	
glass	holds electrons loosely (+)

If two of these materials are rubbed together, for example ebonite and fur, that material that is higher on the list will collect electrons and that material lower on the list will give away electrons. Since ebonite is higher that fur, the ebonite acquires a **net negative charge** (gains electrons, hence excess electrons). The fur loses electrons (hence an electron deficit) and the fur acquires a **net positive charge**. Any object can be charged negatively or positively depending upon the material it is rubbed with.

Electric charge can be transferred from object to object, and from atom to atom within an object. Therefore, all materials are separated into two categories based upon their ability to transfer electrons.

1- **Conductors**: these are materials in which electrons can move easily from atom to atom. Most **metals** are conductors. The electrons can easily move from atom to atom, in fact, so easily that we call these electrons **free electrons**, as they are free to go from atom to atom.

2- **Insulators**: these are materials where the electron movement is restricted. Electrons are *not* free to move from atom to atom. Examples of such materials are wood, plastic, glass, cork, rubber, etc.

All objects may be charged electrically by rubbing. However when a conductor is charged, the net charge will be evenly distributed over the surface of the object. In an insulator, the net charge will be **localized** to the region of the surface that was rubbed.

Once an object is rubbed, it is possible to test if it is electrically charged using an **electroscope**. This is a device that will not only detect the presence of an electric charge, but it will also determine the nature of the charge (+ or -).

There are many different kinds of electroscopes, but the most common is the split-leaf electroscope. It comprises of an insulated (usually glass) container and a central conductor ending in two metallic thin leaves at the bottom.

It is possible to transfer net charge from one object to another by touching (called **conduction**). Usually this is done with conductors, but insulators will also do this. When the knob is touched with an electrically charged object, electrons are transferred to or from the object and to or from the electroscope.

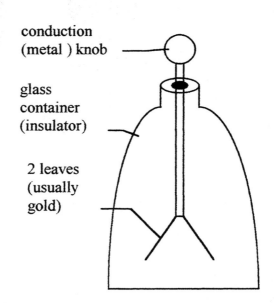

conduction (metal) knob

glass container (insulator)

2 leaves (usually gold)

For example, an ebonite rod is rubbed with fur. The rod gains electrons and is carrying a net negative charge. We say the rod is a negatively charged object. When it is touched to the knob, electrons will leave the rod and move through the conductor giving it a net negative charge. When the electroscope is so charged, the gold leaves *will separate* because each leaf is a negatively charged object and "like objects repel" !

This is shown in a series of diagrams such as this.

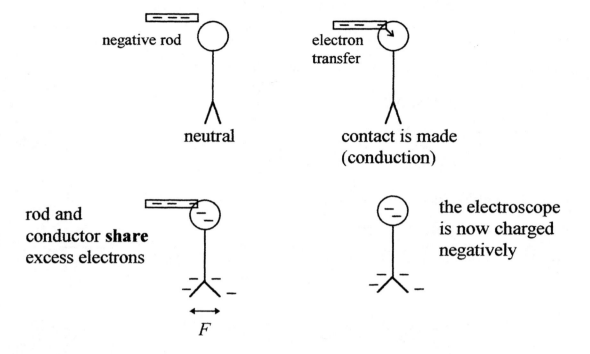

If a glass rod (+) is rubbed with silk, the glass rod may be used to charge an electroscope positively by conduction (contact).

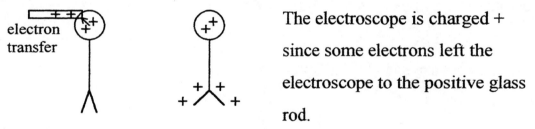

The electroscope is charged + since some electrons left the electroscope to the positive glass rod.

Charging an Object by Induction

When a charged object is brought *near* a neutral object, the charged object can **induce**, or force, a net charge to appear on one side of the object.

PHYSICS GRADE 12

For example:

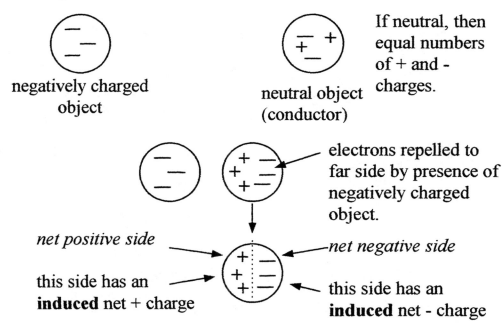

negatively charged
object

neutral object
(conductor)

If neutral, then
equal numbers
of + and -
charges.

electrons repelled to
far side by presence of
negatively charged
object.

net positive side

net negative side

this side has an
induced net + charge

this side has an
induced net - charge

When the negative charge is removed to a large distance, the object will revert back to normal (neutral) as electrons on the far side move back to be with their + protons. *The induced charge is present only while the negative charge is near !* It is because of induction that charged objects attract neutral objects. When a charged object is brought near a neutral object, the opposite charge is induced in the near surface. Then since opposites attract, the neutral (now with a net charge on each side) object will be attracted to the charged object,

negative and positive
objects will attract.

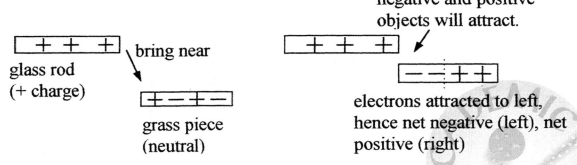

glass rod
(+ charge)

bring near

grass piece
(neutral)

electrons attracted to left,
hence net negative (left), net
positive (right)

PHYSICS GRADE 12

Now, an electroscope can use induction to *detect* the presence of a charge on an object.

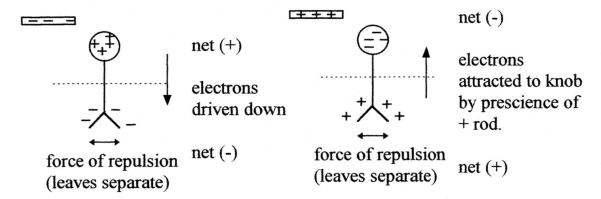

The electroscope, in both cases, is neutral (i.e. no *net* charge).

To use an electroscope to determine the nature (sign) of a charged object, the electroscope must first be given a known charge. By touching the electroscope with a negatively charged ebonite rod, the electroscope will the be negatively charged.

leaves separated

Now, when an unknown charge is brought near to the electroscope, if the unknown charge is negative, it will cause a further separtaion of the leaves. If the unknown charge is positive, it will cause the leaves to collapse.

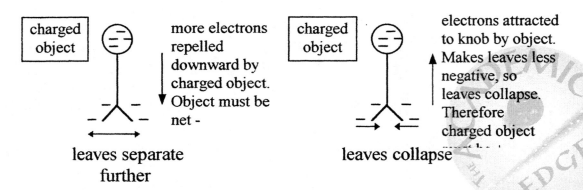

PHYSICS GRADE 12

An object can be charged electrically by induction. When this occurs, the object will have an opposite charge to that of the charging object. To do this we follow this procedure.

1- charged object is brought near a neutral object.

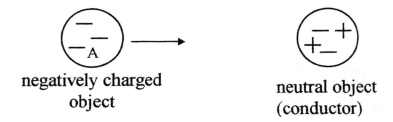

negatively charged
object

neutral object
(conductor)

2- near, but not touching

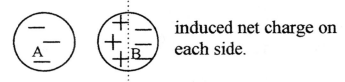

induced net charge on
each side.

3- While charged object A is near neutral object B, touch the far side of the neutral object with your finger.

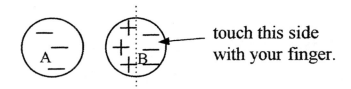

touch this side
with your finger.

Your finger, hand and body give a conduction path for the electrons to enter or leave the neutral object. In the case diagrammed, electrons on right side of neutral object will move through hand to the Earth. The object will then have an electron deficiency once the finger is removed.

4- Remove finger, keeping object near.

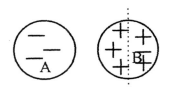

5- Remove charging object.

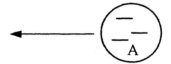 B now charged +
by induction.

Therefore objects can become electrified by a number of methods.

1- by **rubbing** (friction), which causes one object to lose electrons. The other will gain these electrons.

2- by **conduction**: touch the neutral object with a charged object. Both objects share the net charge, therefore both are charged.

3- by **induction**: through this process, a neutral object can be charged with the opposite sign of the charging object.

A few short note concerning charge, charges, charged objects, and electrostatics in general.

• a charged object is often called a **charge**.

• a net charge means more or less electrons that protons.

• all charged objects contain millions of atoms. Each atom contains + and - charges (protons and electrons). Therefore, negatively charged objects will contain some protons. Positively charged objects will contain some electrons. The net charge is simply the *difference* between the total + and total - charges. For example:

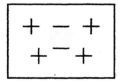   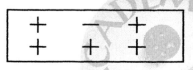

net charge + 2   net charge 0   net charge +4

PHYSICS GRADE 12

This tells us that basically, electricity deals with the redistribution of electrical charges !

Measuring Electric Charge

In 1916, Robert Millikan determined the amount of charge carried by an electron. He determined (through his oil drop experiment) that every net charge on every electrically charged object that he studied carried a charge of **1.6 x 10^{-19} Coulombs**, or some whole numbered multiple of this charge. We use the symbol "q" to denote the net charge on an object. Therefore,

q_e = charge of 1 electron=1.6 x 10^{-19} C (negative electricity).

q_p = charge of 1 proton=1.6 x 10^{-19} C (positive electricity).

q_α = charge of 1 alpha particle=3.2 x 10^{-19} C (positive electricity).

Since each electron carries 1.6 x 10^{-19} C of negative electricity, if we were to gather together 6.25 x 10^{18} electrons, the net charge would be

(6.25 x 10^{18} e)(1.6 x 10^{-19} C/e)= 1 Coulomb = 1C

Electric charge is measured in **Coulombs**.

PHYSICS GRADE 12

Electrical Discharge

Since most objects in this world are electrically neutral, then objects must be able to somehow come back to a balance between - and + charges within. There are a number of ways that electrically charged objects may be neutralized.

1- **Grounding**: because the Earth is a conductor, whenever a charged object come in contact with the Earth, it shares its charge proportionally with size.

a)

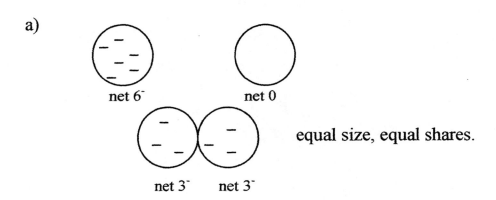

equal size, equal shares.

b)

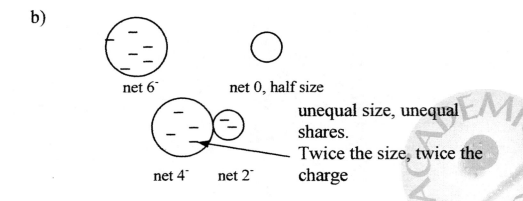

unequal size, unequal shares.
Twice the size, twice the charge

c)

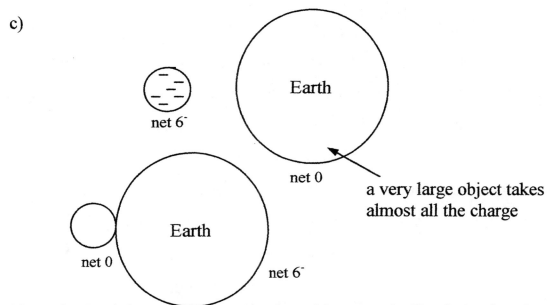

Since the Earth is so large compared to objects on the Earth, it takes the net charge and distributes it evenly over its very large surface. The object then loses its net charge and is neutral. We say the object has been **grounded**. The symbol ⊥ is used to show a path from charged objects to the Earth or **ground**.

  2- **Atmospheric Discharge**: Ions in the air are attracted to objects and can neutralize the object. Moist air contains more ions than dry air, therefore it is difficult to keep charged objects charged on wet, rainy days.

  3- **Sparks**: A charged object may discharge by sending or pulling electrons from some other charged or neutral object. **Lightning** is

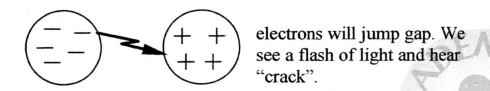

electrons will jump gap. We see a flash of light and hear "crack".

a form of electrical discharge that occurs between clouds and Earth or between clouds.

PHYSICS GRADE 12

Electric Fields

Electric charges will exert forces on each other. These forces can be very strong if the charges are close together. The forces are weak if the charges are separated by a long distance. The force acting between electric charges is called an **electric force** (F_e). To understand how one object can exert a force on another some distance away, you must understand the concepts of **fields**. It is the fields surrounding the charges which actually are responsible for the existence of the electrical forces. The field around a charged object is an **electric field**, $|E|$. It is a **force** field. **Gravitational fields** and **magnetic fields** are other examples of force fields. An electric field is easily understood if it is compared to a gravitational field.

A **gravitational field** is a *region of influence* that surrounds any massive object. It is a region, whereupon a mass when placed there, will experience a gravitational force. Gravitational forces are *always* forces of attraction.

An **electric field** surrounds an electrically charged object. An electric charge in this region will experience an electric force. This force can be attractive or repulsive.

Region of Influence

Gravitational field

Region of Influence

electric field

PHYSICS GRADE 12

Force Laws

F_g = force of gravity

$$F_g = \frac{Gm_1m_2}{R^2}$$

When any to masses come near each other there is a force of attraction acting between them. The above formula (one of Newton's) allows us to calculate the force F_g in **Newtons** if SI units of measure (mks system) are used.

That is m_1 = mass #1 (kg)
$\quad\quad m_2$ = mass #2 (kg)
$\quad\quad G$ = 6.67 x 10^{-11} N m^2/kg^2
$\quad\quad R$ = distance from centre of mass #1 to centre of mass #2. (meters)

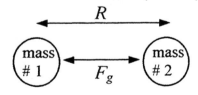

Each mass experiences the same amount of pull. F_g acts equally on both objects. m_1 feels a pull of F_g towards m_2. m_2 experiences the same pull towards m_1. Free of all other forces, these two objects will accelerate toward each other.

F_e = electrical force

$$F_e = \frac{kq_1q_2}{R^2} \quad \textbf{Coulomb's Law}$$

When two electric charges come near each other, the electric force will act between them. This is a force that is attractive between opposite charges, but a force of repulsion between like charges.

That is F_e = electrical force
$\quad\quad q_1$ = electric charge #1 (C)
$\quad\quad q_2$ = electric charge #2 (C)
$\quad\quad k$ = **Coulomb's constant** (constant of variation) = 8.99 x 10^9 N m^2/C^2
$\quad\quad R$ = distance from centre of charge #1 to centre of charge #2. (meters)

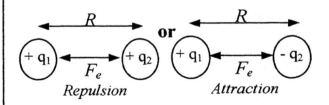

Each charge experiences F_e, that either pushes it towards or pulls it away from the other charge. Free of all other forces, these two objects will accelerate !

If mass #1 is the Earth, we examine the force acting on mass # 2 in terms of the gravitational field of m_1, of the Earth.

$\bigcirc \quad m_2 = 5 \text{ kg}$

field

Earth
m_1
$5.98 \times 10^{24} \text{ kg}$

m_2 is in the region of influence that surrounds the Earth, called a gravitational field. The field has these characteristics.

- it is invisible
- it has no substance, no weight, no smell, no colour, etc.
- its presence can be detected by the mechanical pull it will exert on any mass that is in it.
- theoretically, it extends to infinity with m_1 at its centre.
- such a field exists around every mass.

This force is able to act over a distance because it is actually the interaction of two electric fields of q_1 and q_2.

An electric field surrounds every charged object. The field has the following characteristics.

- it is invisible
- it has no substance, no weight, no smell, no colour, etc., yet it exists in the region surrounding a charged object.
- its presence can be detected by the mechanical push it will exert on any charge that enters the region.
- theoretically, it extends to infinity with q at its centre.
- the field's strength varies inversely with the square of the distance from the centre of q to the point in the field where the strength is to be measured.

- the field varies in its strength, which means that a mass located in the field near to the Earth will experience a large force (strong field), but if far from the Earth, it will experience a much smaller force because of the weaker field.

The strength of the field can be expressed as a ratio of the force exerted on m_2 by the field to the mass of m_2. That is: g is the gravitational field strength at any point in the field where m_2 is located.

$$g = \frac{F_g}{m_2}$$

m_2 is often called a **test mass**. For example, if a 5 kg object experiences a gravitational force of 49 N, then

$$g = \frac{F_g}{m_2} = \frac{49 \text{ N}}{5 \text{ kg}} = 9.8 \text{ N / kg} \quad \text{this}$$

tells us that if any mass is located there, it will experience a

If a **test charge** +, is placed in a field, it will experience an electrical force that will cause it to be pulled towards or pushed away from the charge that is creating the field.

The field is pictorially displayed using **lines of force**. If a charge is free to move in an electric field, it will accelerate along one of these lines. The direction of the force on a positive test charge is defined to be the direction of the electric field. Therefore, electric fields surrounding point charges would look like this.

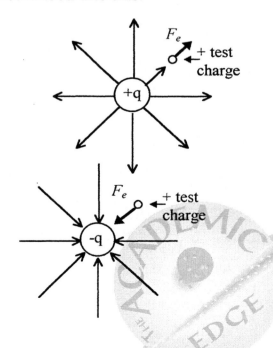

force of 9.8 N for each kg of its mass. This force, exerted by the field of the Earth, will act on any object that is in this region because of the Earth's field.

Often **lines of force** are drawn into the field to show the direction of gravitational forces acting on objects in that field. These imaginary lines give a pictorial representation of a gravitational field.

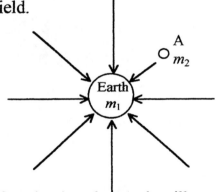

If m_2 is placed at A, it will experience a push towards m_1 along the line of force from A towards m_1. The lines are directed towards the centre of m_1. Since m_2, at A, is a mass, then

$$F_g = \frac{Gm_1m_2}{R^2}$$

The + test charges are used to determine field direction by everyone agreeing that *only* + positive test charges shall be used. **The direction of an electric field is the direction of F_e acting on a + test charge placed in that field**. Therefore a positive charge in an electric field will always experience an electrical force F_e, in the *same direction* as the electric field's direction. A negative charge in the same field will always experience an electrical force in the *opposite* direction to the field's direction.

The strength at any point in an electric field, $|E|$, can be measured using a test charge + of magnitude q. The test charge will be placed into the electric field at the point where $|E|$ is to be measured. F_e will act on q.

and g at A is simply $\dfrac{F_g}{m_2}$

but $g = \dfrac{F_g}{m_2} = \dfrac{\dfrac{Gm_1m_2}{R^2}}{m_2} = \dfrac{Gm_1}{R^2}$.

Expressed like this, g refers to the strength of the gravitational field at A caused by m_1, and measured a distance R from the centre of m_1 to A.

$g = \dfrac{Gm_1}{R^2}$ allows us to find the strength of the gravitational field at R units away from m_1's centre.

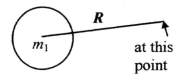

at this point

$g = \dfrac{Gm_1}{R^2}$, G=6.67 x 10^{-4} Nm^2/kg^2

Therefore, $F_g = \dfrac{Gm_1}{R^2} \cdot m_2 = gm_1$

If we know the gravitational field strength of m_1, we can know the force acting on any mass in that field by multiplying the mass by the strength of the gravitational field.

If F_e can be determined, then $|E|$ is simply the ratio of $\dfrac{F_e}{q}$,

therefore $|E| = \dfrac{F_e}{q}$.

Now q=electric charge is measured in units called Coulombs. Since an object acquires a net charge by acquiring a deficit or excess of electrons, it is useful to use electrons to measure charge.

q for 1 electron is 1.6 x 10^{-19} C
q_e=1.6 x 10^{-19} C
Therefore, if an object had

1 excess electron: q= -1.6 x 10^{-19} C
(negative electricity)

2 excess electrons:
q =2(-1.6 x 10^{-19}) C
= -3.2 x 10^{-19} C

2 electron deficit:
q =2(+1.6 x 10^{-19}) C
= +3.2 x 10^{-19} C

Example: A charged object is surrounded by an electric field. A test charge of magnitude 3.2 x 10^{-19}C is placed at point A. This charge experiences a force of repulsion of 9.6 x 10^{-18} N.

Example: A mass of 25 kg is located 40 m above the surface of the Earth. The radius of the Earth is 6.37×10^6 m.

a) How strong is the gravitational force that will act on this mass ?

Use $\quad F_g = \dfrac{Gm_1 m_2}{R^2}$

$R = R_{earth} + 40m + r_{object}$

(centre to centre)

$R \cong$ radius of Earth $= 6.37 \times 10^6$ m

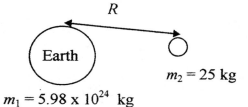

$m_1 = 5.98 \times 10^{24}$ kg

Therefore,

$$F_g = \frac{(6.67 \times 10^{11}\ Nm^2/kg^2)(5.98 \times 10^{24} kg)(25 kg)}{(6.37 \times 10^6\ m)^2}$$

$$= 246\ N$$

Since m_2 experiences 246 N of gravitational pull towards m_1, it will accelerate towards the Earth.

Since $F_{net} = ma$,

$$a = \frac{246\ N}{25\ kg} = 9.8\ m/s^2.$$

What is the strength of the field which the test charge is in ?

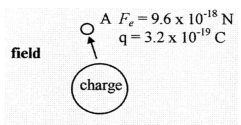

At point A,

$$|E| = \frac{F_e}{q} = \frac{9.6 \times 10^{-18}\ N}{3.2 \times 10^{-19}\ C}$$
$$= 4.0 \times 10^1\ N/C$$

It is convenient to use the magnitude of the charge that is creating the field and the distance from the charge to the point in the field where intensity is to be measured to determine the **electric field intensity** $|E|$. Since F_e acts on the + test charge because of Coulomb's Law,

$$F_e = \frac{kq_1 q_2}{R^2}$$

but $|E| = \dfrac{F_e}{q_2} = \dfrac{\dfrac{kq_1 q_2}{R^2}}{q_2} = \dfrac{kq_1}{R^2}$

This is simply the acceleration due to gravity near the surface of the Earth. Also since

$$g = \frac{F_g}{m_2} = \frac{246 \text{ N}}{25 \text{ kg}} = 9.8 \text{ N} / \text{kg}$$

Near the surface of the Earth, objects accelerate towards the centre of the Earth at 9.81 m/s^2 in a gravitational field of 9.81 N/kg causing the acceleration.

At the same time, the Earth experiences a 246 N pull towards m_2 (caused by m_2's gravitational field).

Since $F=ma$,

$$a = \frac{246 \text{ N}}{5.98 \times 10^{24} \text{ kg}} = 1.70 \times 10^{-25} \text{ m} / \text{s}^2$$

This is the rate at which the earth accelerates towards m_2 .

m_1 accelerates towards m_2 at a very low rate; we do not notice this motion. m_2 accelerates towards m_1 at a much higher rate; we notice m_2 *fall* towards m_1 (the Earth).

This formula is used to find $|E|$ given the magnitude of q_1 and the distance R, the distance from the centre of q_1 to the point in the field where $|E|$ is to be measured.

Once $|E|$ is known, then it is possible to use this value to determine how strong an electrical force would be on a charge (test or otherwise) that is place into that field.

Electric forces act between charges because of the interaction of their fields.

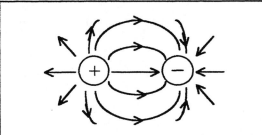

Force of Attraction Between Opposites

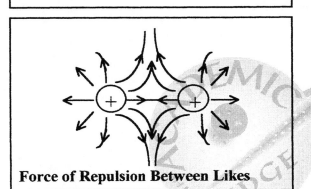

Force of Repulsion Between Likes

The electric field around a point charge varies with the distance from the centre of the charge. Where the lines of force are nearest to each other, the field will be strongest. Where the lines are very far apart, the field will be weak.

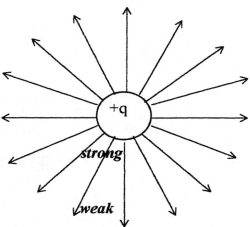

Remember, the lines are imaginary, but they do pictorially represent an electric field. We now know that if a charge is placed on one of these lines, it will experience a force (F_e) directed along one of these lines.

PHYSICS GRADE 12

To review electric fields to this point.

Every charge is surrounded by an electric field. When two charges interact, their fields can cause electric force to act between them. The amount of force on each charge is given by Coulomb's Law.

$$F_e = \frac{kq_1q_2}{R^2}, \text{ where } q_1 \text{ and } q_2 = \text{magnitudes of the charges}$$

R = distance between two charges as measured from the centres

k = Coulomb's constant

Every point charge has an electric field around it. To determine the strength of the field at any point in the field, we can do one of two things.

1- Measure the distance from the center of the charge to the point in the field where the electric field intensity is to be measured.

$$|E| = \frac{kq}{R^2}, \quad \text{where} \qquad q = \text{magnitudes of the charge}$$

creating the field

R = distance from centre to field point

k = Coulomb's constant

or   **2-**Place a test charge q into the field, it will experience an electric force (F_e), then $|E| = \dfrac{F_e}{q}$.

A third means of measuring electric field strength involves determining the field's ability to do work. Again, a comparison to gravitational fields is useful.

In order to do work on mass *m* and move it away from the Earth in the Earth's gravitational field, we have to exert a force on *m* = weight of *m* against the gravitational force. Therefore, ***F=mg.*** When we move *m* from A to B, we do work.

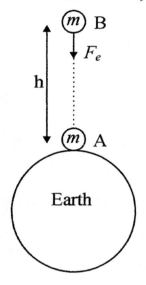

W=*Fd*   but   *F=mg,*

therefore

$$W=mgh.$$

The work done against the gravitational field is now stored as gravitational potential energy in the Earth-mass system. This change (gain) in PE can be recovered by letting B return back to A.

So   ΔPE=*mgh.*

The mass is in a region of high potential energy at B, but low potential energy at A.

In a similar fashion, suppose we have a large negative object on which sits a small positive object.

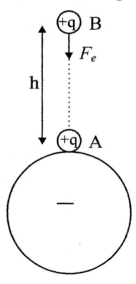

To move the + object through the electric field of the negative charge, we must exert a force= F_e on the positive charge in the opposite direction to the electric force exerted by the field on +.

The work done to move the charge from A to B is $W = F_e \, d.$

but $F_e = q|E|,$

where $|E|$ is the strength of the electric field.

Therefore $W = q|E|d$.   This work goes to raise the electric potential energy of +, and can be recovered if + is released at B. At B, + is at a high potential energy, but + is at low potential energy at A. We say there is **a potential energy difference** between points A and B in the field of the negative charge.

Therefore $\Delta PE = q|E|d$. If we know the ΔPE experienced by a charge q as it is moved through an electric field between points A and B, we can determine the quantity known as the **electric potential difference**, or simply th**e potential difference** between these two points by the ratio of

$$V = \frac{\Delta PE}{q},$$

where V = potential difference measured in Volts.
q=charge of the object being moved in that field.

Now, $|E|$ surrounding a point charge *varies* with the distance from the charge creating $|E|$. Therefore it is difficult to determine V between point in fields of point charges. If two charged plates are used, we then obtain a **uniform electric field** where $|E|$ is constant at all points in that field.

For example,

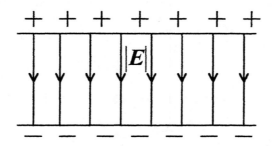

Now, suppose a positive charge was sitting on the bottom plate.

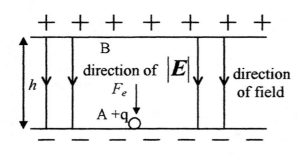

To move the charge from A to B requires a constant force $=F_e$, but $F_e = q|E|$. If the positive charge is pushed upwards, then the work done is

$$W = F_e \, d$$
$$W = qEd$$

The charge q (positive) gains PE. When it is at B, it has high PE. If released at B, it would experience an electric force (F_e) that would accelerate it towards A. Now suppose that $E = 3.4 \times 10^5$ N/C, $q = 5.6 \times 10^{-6}$ C, and $d = 0.5$ m. Then the work to move +q from A to B is

$$W = F_e \, d$$
$$W = qEd$$
$$= (5.6 \times 10^{-6} \text{ C})(3.4 \times 10^5 \text{ N/C})(0.5\text{m})$$
$$= 9.52 \times 10^{-1} \text{ J}$$
$$= \text{PE gain for q} = \Delta\text{PE}$$

We can determine the potential difference between A and B from

$$V = \frac{\Delta PE}{q} = \frac{9.52 \times 10^{-1} \text{ J}}{5.6 \times 10^{-6} \text{ C}} = 1.7 \times 10^5 \text{ J} / \text{C} = 1.7 \times 10^5 \text{ Volts.}$$

The potential difference tells us the amount of work that the field will do on a unit charge in moving the charge between two points in the field. Or, the amount of work needed to move a unit charge against the field between the two points. For example, a potential difference of 1.7×10^5 V between points A and B means that 1.7×10^5 J of work are needed to move 1 C of charge between A and B. If you move a 1 C charge from *A to B*, you must do 1.7×10^5 J of work against the field; the field can do 1.7×10^5 J of work in moving a 1 C charge from *B to A*.

The electric potential difference that exists across two charged plates is measured with a device called a **voltmeter**. Once V is known, then $|E|$ can be determined

Since
$$V = \frac{\Delta PE}{q} = \frac{q|E|d}{q},$$

$$V = |E|d$$

and
$$|E| = \frac{V}{d}.$$

We use this method to determine the electric field intensity between two charged plates separated by a distance *d*, when a potential difference of V volts exists across them.

PHYSICS GRADE 12

We use this method to determine the electric field intensity between two charged plates separated by a distance d, when a potential difference of V volts exists across them.

Example: Find the $|E|$ between two unlike charged plates separated by 20 cm, if the potential difference measured across the plates is 220 V.

Answer: Since $|E| = \dfrac{V}{d} = \dfrac{220 \text{ V}}{0.20 \text{ m}} = 1.1 \text{ x } 10^3 \text{ V / m}$

1 V/m = 1 N/C,

therefore $|E| = 1.1 \text{ x } 10^3$ N/C

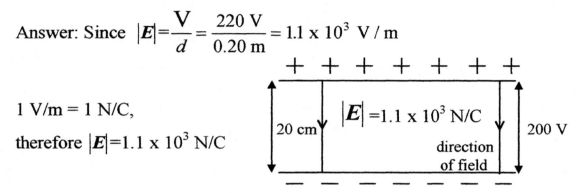

Electric Charges in Electric Fields

If an electric charge is in an electric field, it will experience an electric force, F_e. If the charge is free of all other forces, then F_e is the net force acting on the charge. Therefore, the charge will accelerate in the direction of F_e. ***An electric charge in an electric field and free of all other forces will accelerate***.

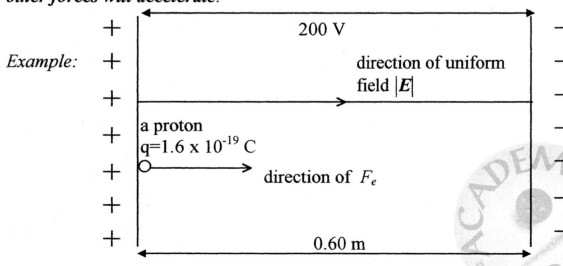

A proton is placed in the electric field between two oppositely charged plates. The proton will experience a push away from the positive plate and a pull toward the negative plate.

a) What is the strength of $|E|$ between the plates ?

Answer: $|E| = \dfrac{V}{d} = \dfrac{200 \text{ V}}{0.60 \text{ m}} = 3.3 \times 10^2$ V / m or 3.3×10^2 N / C

b) How strong is the electric force that will push the proton to the negative plate ?

Answer: $F_e = q|E|$ (since $|E| = \dfrac{F_e}{q}$)

$\quad\quad\quad = (1.6 \times 10^{-19} \text{ C})(3.3 \times 10^2 \text{ N/C})$

$\quad\quad\quad = 5.3 \times 10^{-17}$ N

c) If F_e is the only force acting on q, then at what rate will q accelerate across the electric field ?

Answer: Since $F_{net} = ma$,

$\quad\quad$ then $F_e = ma$

$\quad\quad$ and $a = \dfrac{F_e}{m} = \dfrac{5.3 \times 10^{-17} \text{ N}}{1.67 \times 10^{-27} \text{ kg}} = 3.2 \times 10^{10}$ m / s^2

d) How much work does the field do on q in moving the charge from the positive plate to the negative plate ?

Answer: $W = F_e\, d$

$\quad\quad\quad = (5.3 \times 10^{-17} \text{ N})(0.60 \text{ m})$

$\quad\quad\quad = 3.2 \times 10^{-17}$ J

e) What is the kinetic energy gain for the proton in moving from the +plate to the - plate ?

Answer: $KE_{gain} = \text{Work} = 3.2 \times 10^{-17}$ J

---

f) What is the speed of the proton when it reached the -plate, if it starts from rest at the +plate ?

Answer: Since $KE = \dfrac{1}{2}mv^2$,

$$\text{then } v = \sqrt{\frac{2KE}{m}} = \sqrt{\frac{2(3.2 \times 10^{-17} \text{ J})}{1.67 \times 10^{-27} \text{ kg}}} = \sqrt{3.8 \times 10^{10} \frac{\text{m}^2}{\text{s}^2}}$$

$$= 1.95 \times 10^5 \text{ m/s}$$

g) Use Kinematics to determine the speed of the proton after traveling across the electric field.

Answer: Since $a = 3.2 \times 10^{10}$ m/s^2, and the object accelerates at this uniform rate over a distance of 0.60 m, then

$$v_f{}^2 = v_i{}^2 + 2ad$$
$$= 0 + 2(3.2 \times 10^{10} \text{ m/s}^2)(0.60 \text{ m})$$
$$= 3.8 \times 10^{10} \text{ m/s}^2$$
$$v_f = 1.96 \times 10^5 \text{ m/s}$$

Remember

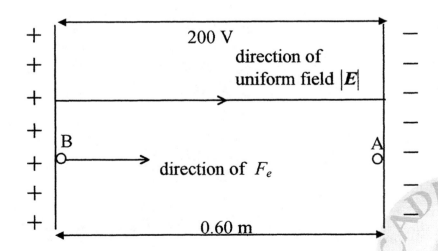

To move the positive charge from A to B, work must be done against the field (this is like lifting a rock against the force of gravity). At B, the

PHYSICS GRADE 12

To move the positive charge from A to B, work must be done against the field (this is like lifting a rock against the force of gravity). At B, the +charge has potential energy (from A to B it gains PE). IF the +charge is released at B, it will fall towards A. The electric field will do work on the +charge, and it will lose PE and gain KE as it moves towards A (the rock has PE gain as it is raised, but loses PE and gains KE as it falls towards the Earth).

For a *positive* charge in the field,

         A to B   gain PE

         B to A   lose PE (gain KE)

For a *negative* charge in the field,

         A to B   lose PE (gain KE)

         B to A   gain PE   because it experiences F_e in the opposite direction.

Since $V = \dfrac{\Delta PE}{q}$, then $\Delta PE = qV$

or simply $\boxed{\text{Energy Change} = q\,V \quad \text{or} \quad E = q\,V}$

The energy change can be measured as a potential energy gain or loss, or a kinetic energy gain or loss.

       To return to question *e)*

e) What is the kinetic energy gain from the proton in moving from the +plate to the - plate ?

Answer: $KE_{gain} = q\,V$ $= (1.6 \times 10^{-19} \text{ C})(200 \text{ V})$
                              $= 3.2 \times 10^{-17} \text{ J}$

If an electron or proton falls through a potential difference of V volts, and the charge carried by 1 electron (-) or one proton (+) is 1e, then

If an electron or proton falls through a potential difference of V volts, and the charge carried by 1 electron (-) or one proton (+) is 1e, then

$$KE_{gain} = q\,V = (1e)(200\ V)$$
$$= 200\ eV$$

The eV, or **electron-volt** is a very small unit of energy. An electron falling across a potential difference of 1 volt will gain 1 eV of KE.

$$\boxed{1\ eV = 1.6 \times 10^{-19}\ J}$$ *Remember this conversion factor.*

Electric Currents and Circuits

Whenever an electric charge moves, it is an electric current. Electric current is measured in **Amperes** (A), and uses the symbol I. The Ampere is a **basic unit** in physics. If, in a beam of electrons, a total amount of charge, q, passes a given point in space per unit time, then

$$I = \frac{q}{t}.$$

If q is measured in Coulombs, and t is measured in seconds, then I is measured in Amperes; 1 Ampere = 1 C/s.

It was noticed that electric charges could be transferred through conductors over 200 years ago, but it was not until 1800 **when Alessandro Volta** developed the first electrochemical cell that would supply a continuous electric current, or **flow** of electrons, so that electric currents could be seriously studied. Volta found that if two dissimilar metals were placed together with a salt bridge between them, one metal would acquire a +charge, and the other a -charge.

For example, silver and zinc!

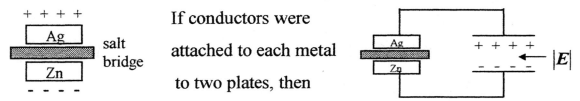

salt bridge

If conductors were attached to each metal to two plates, then

If conductor is attached in a continuous fashion, then $|E|$ exists in the conductor and electrons flow from zinc to silver along the external path.

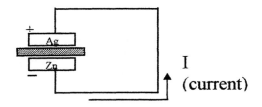

I (current)

The zinc-silver cell can be connected to other cells to form a battery. The battery is a source of potential difference. This device does work by separating + and - charge. The work goes to increase the PE of the electrons removed from their associated protons. The energy necessary for this work comes from stored chemical energy that is released through a chemical reaction. The battery converts this chemical energy into electrical potential energy.

Today we have other devices which will do the work necessary to separate + and - charges.

    1- electric generator

    2- photoelectric cells

    3- many kinds of batteries

Whatever the device, **a source of potential difference**, converts some form of energy into electric potential energy of electrons. When the + terminal and -terminal are connected by a conductor, the -

charges can return to + around this external path. We then form an **electric circuit**.

Every electric circuit has these three components

1- a source of potential (V)

2- a resistance (R)

3- an electric current (I)

In a diagram, called a **schematic diagram**, we see an electric circuit shown like this

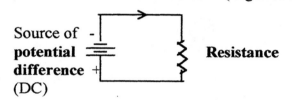

I **current flow** (negative charge flow)

Source of potential difference (DC)   Resistance

The source of potential difference puts energy into the circuit and drives electrons around the circuit, always from - to +. The **resistance** (or **load**) is some device that converts electrical potential energy into heat, light sound,. etc. (some other form). The current carries the energy from V to R.

A "D" cell alkaline battery is rated at 1.5 Volts.

Because 1.5 V= 1.5 J/C, then this battery will supply 1.5 J of energy for each Coulomb of charge that it separates.

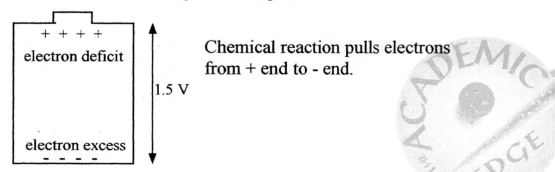

+ + + +
electron deficit

1.5 V

electron excess
- - - -

Chemical reaction pulls electrons from + end to - end.

Electrons (believed to be easily moved, while protons are believed to be fixed in position) driven to the negative terminal cannot return back to + end internally, but they may do so externally.

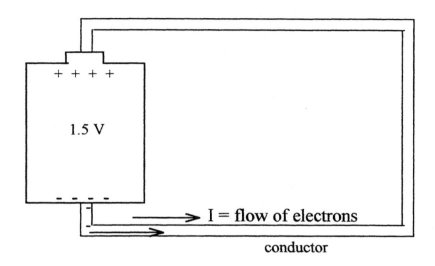

I = flow of electrons

conductor

When the conductor is connected to the terminals of the battery, one end of the conductor is -, and the other is +.

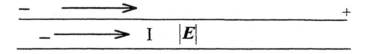

An electric field in the conductor will cause F_e to push electrons towards the + end, and electron current will flow. If the conductor was a vacuum, the electrons would accelerate towards the + terminal, losing PE and gaining KE. However, in a conductor there are atoms for the electron to collide with. An electron will accelerate for a while then bump onto an atom in the conductor. Some of its KE will be transferred to the atom, increasing the KE of the atom. As the average KE of the atoms in the conductor increases, we would notice this as an increase in temperature of the conductor. In other words, the current will cause the conductor to heat up. If the conductor gets very hot, like the filament in a light bulb, it can emit light!

We say the atoms offer resistance to the flow of electrons. All conductors do this. But most conductors are **good conductors**, and their resistance to the flow of electrons is small. The resistance of a conductor to an electric current depends upon;

1- material used for the conductor

All metals offer low resistance, but some are better than others. The lower the resistance the conductor has, the greater the amount of energy available to the load. Silver, copper, and aluminum are all very good, low resistance conductors, and are often found in ordinary household wiring.

2- cross-section area of the conductor

Area

The larger the area, the less resistance.

3- length of the conductor

The longer the conductor, the greater the resistance.

4- temperature

The lower the temperature, the lower the resistance.

Theoretically, at absolute zero (0 k), **no resistance**!

In most circuits, a device that offers a high resistance (called a load) is inserted into the circuit. This could be a light bulb, toaster, hairdryer, radio, television etc. This device will be constructed so that it takes the potential energy of the electrons given to them by the source of potential difference, and converts that energy into a more useful form of energy.

PHYSICS GRADE 12

Simple Electric Circuit

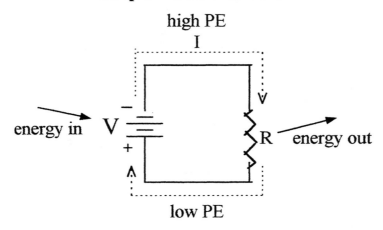

At V, electric potential gain for electrons.

At R, electric potential energy *drop*.

The current; $I \propto V$ but $I \propto \dfrac{1}{R}$

therefore $I = \dfrac{V}{R}$ or $\boxed{V = IR}$ **Ohm's Law**

V is measured in Volts (V)
I is measured in Amperes (A)
R is measured in ohms (Ω)
(Ω is the Greek letter **omega**)

To determine the resistance of the conductor, an **ohm meter** may be used.

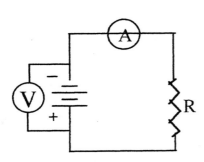

A voltmeter is used to find the potential difference across the ends of the conductor. An ammeter is inserted into the circuit to measure the current.

Then $R = \dfrac{V}{I}$ by ohm's law.

So the current in a simple circuit where $V = 6$ Volts and $R = 24 \, \Omega$ is

$$I = \dfrac{V}{R} = \dfrac{6 \, V}{24 \, \Omega} = 0.25 \, A$$

At times, more than one load is in a circuit. They may be connected in series, parallel or a combination of the two.

Series Circuit

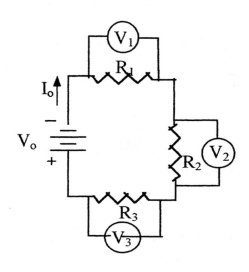

In this circuit, the current I must be the same through all the resistors.

Therefore $I_o = I_1 = I_2 = I_3$

where

I_o = current in circuit
I_1 = current through resistor 1

I_2 = current through resistor 2

etc.

Also the total resistance of the circuit is

$$R_T = R_1 + R_2 + R_3$$

therefore

$$I_o = \dfrac{V_o}{R_T}$$

There will be a potential energy drop as electrons flow through R_1. The drop across R_1 can be measured by a voltmeter (equal to V_1), and

$$V_o = V_1 + V_2 + V_3$$

but at V_o, there's an electric potential energy gain, and at V_1, V_2, V_3, an electric potential energy drop.

Parallel Circuits

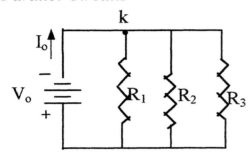

Since current has different paths to take at k, some current will separate at k, and move through R_1 ; The rest of the current will pass on to R_2 and R_3. Since potential difference is the same in any complete loop.

So $$V_o = V_1 = V_2 = V_3,$$

and $$I_o = I_1 + I_2 + I_3$$

to find R_T, we know that $\dfrac{I_o}{V_o} = \dfrac{1}{R_T}$

but $$\frac{I_o}{V_o} = \frac{I_1 + I_2 + I_3}{V_o}$$

and $$\frac{I_o}{V_o} = \frac{I_1}{V_o} + \frac{I_2}{V_o} + \frac{I_3}{V_o}$$

but since $V_o = V_1 = V_2 = V_3,$

then $$\frac{I_o}{V_o} = \frac{I_1}{V_1} + \frac{I_2}{V_2} + \frac{I_3}{V_3}$$

and $$\frac{1}{R_T} = \frac{1}{R_1} + \frac{1}{R_2} + \frac{1}{R_3}$$

Example: *For a combination circuit, find the current through each resistor and the potential energy drop across each resistor.*

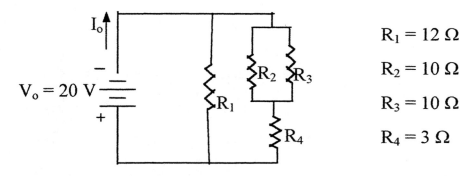

$R_1 = 12 \ \Omega$

$R_2 = 10 \ \Omega$

$R_3 = 10 \ \Omega$

$R_4 = 3 \ \Omega$

Answer: Since 20 V exists across R_1, then $I_1 = \dfrac{V}{R_1} = \dfrac{20 \ V}{12 \ \Omega} = 1.67 \ A$.

Total resistance of circuit:

Notice that R_2 is parallel to R_3. Therefore these two resistors can be replaced by one resistance R,

$\dfrac{1}{R} = \dfrac{1}{R_2} + \dfrac{1}{R_3}$

$\dfrac{1}{R} = \dfrac{1}{10 \ \Omega} + \dfrac{1}{10 \ \Omega} = \dfrac{2}{10 \ \Omega}$

$R = \dfrac{10}{2} \Omega = 5 \ \Omega$

Now R and R_4 are in series:

$R = 5 \ \Omega + 3 \ \Omega$
$\quad = 8 \ \Omega$

Now these two resistors are in parallel, therefore:

$\dfrac{1}{R_T} = \dfrac{1}{R_1} + \dfrac{1}{R}$

$$\frac{1}{R_T} = \frac{1}{12\,\Omega} + \frac{1}{8\,\Omega} = \frac{2}{24\,\Omega} + \frac{3}{24\,\Omega}$$

$$= \frac{5}{24\,\Omega}$$

$$R_T = \frac{24}{5}\,\Omega = 4.8\,\Omega$$

and $\quad I_o = \dfrac{V_o}{R_T} = \dfrac{20\text{ V}}{4.8\,\Omega} = 4.17\text{ A}$

since $I_1 = 1.67$ A, then $I_4 = 2.5$ A

Since $V_{gain} = V_{loss}$ around any loop, then V across R_2 and R_3 + V across

R_4 must equal 20 V.

$$V_4 = I_4\,R_4$$
$$= (2.5\text{ A})(3\,\Omega)$$
$$= 7.5\text{ Volts}$$

Therefore, the potential drop across R_2 and $R_3 = (20\text{ V} - 7.5\text{ V}) = 12.5$ V,

so $\quad I_2 = \dfrac{V_2}{R_2} = \dfrac{12.5\text{ V}}{10\,\Omega} = 1.25\text{ A} \quad$ and $\quad I_3 = \dfrac{V_3}{R_3} = \dfrac{12.5\text{ V}}{10\,\Omega} = 1.25\text{ A}$

We have

$V_o, V_1, V_2, V_3, V_4 = 20$ V, 20 V, 12.5 V, 12.5 V, 7.5 V

$I_o, I_1, I_2, I_3, I_4 = 4.17$ A, 1.67 A, 1.25 A, 1,25 A, 2.50 A

$R_o, R_1, R_2, R_3, R_4 = 4.8\,\Omega$, 12 Ω, 10 Ω, 10 Ω, 3 Ω

Notice:

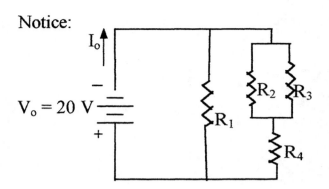

notice *two* loops here,

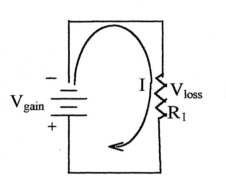

replace with
single resistor

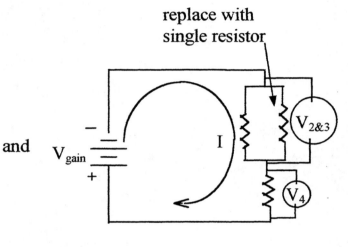

therefore $V = V_1$

and

$V = V_{2 \text{ and } 3} + V_4$

gain $=$ loss $+$ loss

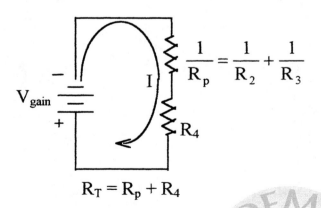

$R_T = R_p + R_4$

Keep in mind, Kirchoff's Law, when annalyzing electric circuits.

1. The voltage gains around a circuit loop = the voltage drops.

2. The current into a junction = the current out of the junction.

In any electric circuit, energy is put into the circuit at the source of potential difference and it is removed at each load, or resistance. The power rating of a load is the rate at which energy is delivered to the load, or rate at which energy is consumed by the load.

The source of potential difference adds a certain amount of PE to each Coulomb of charge it separates. The electrons then carry this energy by a current to the load. The current is, of course, "so many" C/s. Therefore, if

$$V = \frac{energy}{charge} \quad \text{and} \quad I = \frac{charge}{time}$$

then

$$\boxed{power = P = VI}$$

so

$$power = \frac{energy}{charge} \cdot \frac{charge}{time} = \frac{energy}{time}$$

Since $V = IR$, then

$$P = (IR)I$$

$$\boxed{P = I^2 R}$$

or since $I = \dfrac{V}{R}$, then

$$P = V \cdot \left(\frac{V}{R}\right)$$

$$\boxed{P = \frac{V^2}{R}}$$

Power rates can be determined from any of the above equations.

Since P= energy/time, energy consumption = Pt.

And since P = VI, then

$$E = V \; It$$

Example: *How much energy does a 110 V electric kettle use in 2 minutes, if it draws a current of 8.0 A ?*

Answer: $E = V \; It$ but I is measured in C/s, therefore t
                                          must be in seconds.

$$E = (110 \text{ V})(8.0 \text{ A})(120 \text{ s})$$
$$= (110 \text{ J/C})(8.0 \text{ C/s})(120 \text{ s})$$
$$= 1.06 \times 10^5 \text{ J}$$

PHYSICS GRADE 12

Electricity and Electric Fields Solved Problems

1. If two charges of magnitudes 3.0 x 10^{-5} C and 5.0 x 10^{-4} C attract with a force of 3.8 x 10^3 N, then what is the separation of the charges ?

Answer: use Coulomb's law: $F_e = \dfrac{kq_1q_2}{R^2}$

then $R =$ distance separating the charges

$$R = \sqrt{\dfrac{kq_1q_2}{F_e}}$$

$$= \sqrt{\dfrac{(8.99 \times 10^9 \, \text{N} \, \text{m}^2 \, / \, \text{C}^2)(3.0 \times 10^{-5} \, \text{C})(5 \times 10^{-4} \, \text{C})}{(3.8 \times 10^3 \, \text{N})}}$$

$$= \sqrt{35.5 \times 10^{-3} \, \text{m}^2}$$

$$= \sqrt{3.55 \times 10^{-2}} \, \text{m}$$

$$= 1.88 \times 10^{-1} \, \text{m}$$

$$= \mathbf{0.19 \ m}$$

2. What is the weight of a 50 kg alien on Uranus, if the planet has a mass of 8.80 x 10^{25} kg, and a radius of 2.67 x 10^7 m ?

Answer: Since weight is a measure of the force of gravity $= F_g$ acting on

the   object, then weight $= F_g = mg$, but on Uranus, g is

$$g = \dfrac{Gm}{R^2} = \dfrac{(6.67 \times 10^{-11} \, \dfrac{\text{Nm}^2}{\text{kg}^2})(8.80 \times 10^{25} \, \text{kg})}{(2.67 \times 10^7 \, \text{m})^2}$$

$$= 8.23 \times 10^0 \, \text{N/kg}$$

therefore,   weight $= F_g = mg$

$$= (50 \ \text{kg})(8.23 \ \text{N/kg}) = \mathbf{411.5 \ N}$$

PHYSICS GRADE 12

3. *What is the force on a negative charge of 5.4 x 10⁻³ C that is in an electric field of intensity 6.5 x 10⁵ N/C ?*

Answer: Since $F_e = q|E|$

then $F_e = (5.4 \times 10^{-3} \, C)(6.5 \times 10^5 \, N/C)$

$= \mathbf{3.5 \times 10^3 \, N}$

4. *What is the potential difference across two plates that are separated by 5 cm, if the electric field intensity between the plates is 5.8 x 10³ N/C ?*

Answer: Since $|E| = V/d$

then $V = |E|d$

$= (5.8 \times 10^3 \, N/C)(5 \times 10^{-2} \, m)$
$= 29 \times 10^1 \, Nm/C$
$= 2.9 \times 10^2 \, J/C$
$= \mathbf{2.9 \times 10^2 \, V}$

5. *A lithium nucleus with a +3e charge and a sodium nucleus with a charge of +11e are separated by a distance of 4.6 x 10⁻⁶ m. What is the force of repulsion acting between them ?*

Answer: Since this is an electrostatic force (F_e), use Coulomb's law.

$$F_e = \frac{kq_1q_2}{R^2}$$

$$= \frac{(8.99 \times 10^9 \, N \, m^2 / C^2)(3 \times 1.6 \times 10^{-19} \, C)(11 \times 1.6 \times 10^{-19} \, C)}{(4.6 \times 10^{-6} \, m)^2}$$

$= 35.9 \times 10^{-17} \, N$
$= 3.59 \times 10^{-16} \, N$
$= \mathbf{3.6 \times 10^{-16} \, N}$

6. *A 6 V battery supplies a circuit with a current of 2.5 A. What is the number of electrons passing a point in the circuit in 5 s ?*

Answer: The current tells us the amount of charge passing a point each

second. That is,

$$2.5 \text{ A} = 2.5 \text{ C/s}$$

since $I = q/t$

then $q = It$

$$= (2.4 \text{ A})(5 \text{ s})$$

$$= (2.4 \text{ C/s})(5 \text{ s})$$

$$= 12.5 \text{ C}$$

therefore 12.5 C passes a point in 5 s.

The number of electrons required to make a charge of 12.5 C

is

$$\frac{12.5 \text{ C}}{1.6 \times 10^{-19} \text{ C}/e} = \textbf{7.8} \times \textbf{10}^{\textbf{19}} \textbf{ e}$$

7. *If a heating element conducts 7.5 A when it radiates heat at the rate of 1.2×10^3 W, then what is the voltage across the heating element ?*

Answer: Since $P = VI$

then

$$V = \frac{P}{I} = \frac{1.2 \times 10^3 \text{ W}}{7.5 \text{ A}}$$

$$= \frac{1.2 \times 10^3 \text{ J}/\text{s}}{7.5 \text{ C}/\text{s}}$$

$$= \textbf{160 Volts}$$

8. *At a distance of 0.60 m from a $+3.4 \times 10^{-4}$ C charge, what is the intensity and the direction of the electric field ?*

Answer: $|E| = \dfrac{kq}{R^2} = \dfrac{(8.99 \times 10^9 \text{ Nm}^2/\text{C}^2)(3.4 \times 10^{-4}\text{ C})}{(0.60\text{ m})^2}$

$$= 84.9 \times 10^5 \text{ N/C}$$

$$= \mathbf{8.5 \times 10^6 \text{ N/C}}$$

Direction: always *away* from a +charge.

9. *What will be the speed of an electron that accelerates from rest through a potential difference of 3.0×10^2 V ?*

Answer: Since $\quad E = qV$

then $\quad KE = (1.6 \times 10^{-19}\text{ C})(3.0 \times 10^2\text{ V})$

$$= 4.8 \times 10^{-17}\text{ J}$$

Since $\quad KE = mv^2/2$

$$v = \sqrt{\dfrac{2KE}{m}} = \sqrt{\dfrac{2(4.6 \times 10^{-12}\text{ J})}{9.11 \times 10^{-31}\text{ kg}}} = \sqrt{1.05 \times 10^{14}}\text{ m/s}$$

$$= \mathbf{1.02 \times 10^7 \text{ m/s}}$$

10. *An electric crane lifts a 35 kg mass to a height of 12 m in 8.0 s. If the motor draws a current of 6.0 A, and is 100% efficient, what is the minimum possible voltage that could be applied to the motor ?*

Answer: Since   power output $= \dfrac{\text{work}}{\text{time}} = \dfrac{F_g \times d}{t}$

and since $F_g = mg$,

$$P = \dfrac{mgd}{t}$$

$$= \dfrac{(35 \text{ kg})(9.81 \text{ N / kg})(12 \text{ m})}{8.0 \text{ s}}$$

$$= 515 \text{ W}$$

Since 100% efficient, then this same power must be available

for input.

Therefore,

input power$= VI$

and $V = \dfrac{P}{I} = \dfrac{515 \text{ W}}{6.0 \text{ A}} = 85.8 \text{ V}$

$$= \mathbf{86 \text{ V}}$$

PHYSICS GRADE 12

Electricity and Electric Fields Practice Problems

1. What is the electric force acting between two charges of $+4.5 \times 10^{-6}$ C and -3.8×10^{-6} C when they are separated by a distance of 10 m ?

2. A charge of magnitude 6.2×10^{-4} C is placed into an electric field where it experiences a force of 2.1×10^{2} N. What is the electric field intensity at the point where the force was measured ?

3. An α-particle is placed in the electric field between two charged plates separated by a distance of 6.2×10^2 cm. If the voltage across the plates is 1.8×10^2 V, what is the rate of acceleration of the α-particle ?

4. If the distance between the plates in question 3 is halved, and the α-particle is replaced by a proton, the what is the new rate of acceleration ?

5. Three charges A, B, and C with charges respectively of $+3.2 \times 10^{-6}$ C, $+4.4 \times 10^{-6}$ C, and -7.8×10^{-6} C are placed as seen in the diagram. What is the force on B because of A and C ?

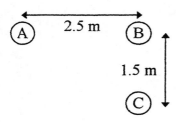

6. A radar set operates on 24 V and draws a current of 12 Amperes. How much energy does it use in a 24 hour period ?

7. If the cost of the energy is $0.03 per kJ, what is the cost of operating the radar set in question 6 for 24 hours ?

8. Two conducting spheres with charges of $+3.2 \times 10^{-6}$ C and -4.8×10^{-6} C are touched together and the separated by a distance of 3.4 m. What is the magnitude of the force acting on each charge ?

9.

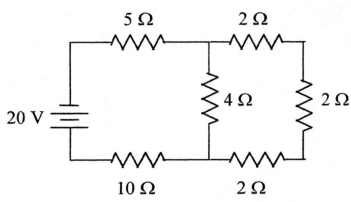

a) Find the total resistance of the circuit.

b) Find the current through each resistor.

10. It requires an average force of 6.00×10^{-3} N to move a 3.3×10^{-3} C charge from one point in an electric field to another point that is 1.2 m away. What is the potential difference between the two points ?

11. On planet X, with mass 6.4×10^{34} kg, a 30 kg skwib weighs 742 N. What is the radius of the planet ?

12. A proton accelerates through a distance of 5.0 cm in an electric field of intensity 4.4×10^1 N/C. What will its final speed be, if it starts from rest?

13. A charged oil drop has a mass of 3.6×10^{-12} kg, and it is suspended in an electric field of intensity 3.5×10^4 N/C. What is the charge in the oil drop ?

14. What is the number of electrons needed to give the oil drop in question 13 the charge you calculated ?

PHYSICS GRADE 12

Electricity and Electric Fields Practice Problem Solutions

1. What is the electric force acting between two charges of $+4.5 \times 10^{-6}$ C and -3.8×10^{-6} C when they are separated by a distance of 10 m ?

Answer: Use Coulomb's Law

$$F_e = \frac{kq_1q_2}{R^2}$$

$$= \frac{(8.99 \times 10^9 \, N \, m^2/C^2)(4.5 \times 10^{-6} \, C)(3.8 \times 10^{-6} \, C)}{(10 \, m)^2}$$

$$= \textbf{1.53 x 10}^{\textbf{-3}} \textbf{ N} \text{ (force of attraction)}$$

2. A charge of magnitude 6.2×10^{-4} C is placed into an electric field where it experiences a force of 2.1×10^2 N. What is the electric field intensity at the point where the force was measured ?

Answer: Since $\quad |E| = \dfrac{F}{q} = \dfrac{2.1 \times 10^2 \, N}{6.2 \times 10^{-4} \, C} = 0.34 \times 10^6 \, N/C$

$$= \textbf{3.4 x 10}^{\textbf{5}} \textbf{ N/C}$$

3. *An α-particle is placed in the electric field between two charged plates separated by a distance of 6.2 x 10² cm. If the voltage across the plates is 1.8 x 10² V, what is the rate of acceleration of the α-particle ?*

Answer: Electric field strength between plates is

$$|\mathbf{E}| = \frac{V}{d} = \frac{1.8 \times 10^2 \, V}{6.2 \, m} = 0.29 \times 10^2 \, V/m$$

$$= 2.9 \times 10^1 \, V/m \text{ or } (N/C).$$

Electric force will act on α-particle,

$$F_e = q_\alpha |\mathbf{E}| = (3.2 \times 10^{-19} \, C)(2.9 \times 10^1 \, N/C) = 9.28 \times 10^{-18} \, N$$

Since this is the *net* force, then

$$a = \frac{F_{net}}{m} = \frac{9.28 \times 10^{-18} \, N}{6.65 \times 10^{-27} \, kg} = \mathbf{1.40 \times 10^9 \; m/s^2}$$

4. *If the distance between the plates in question 3 is halved, and the α-particle is replaced by a proton, the what is the new rate of acceleration ?*

Answer: Since $\quad a = \dfrac{F_{net}}{m} = \dfrac{F_e}{m} = \dfrac{q|\mathbf{E}|}{m} = \dfrac{q\left(\dfrac{V}{d}\right)}{m} = \dfrac{qV}{md}$

then q is 1/2, since q for a proton is +1e, while q for alpha-particle   is +2e.

Then new $\quad a = \dfrac{\left(\dfrac{1}{2}q\right)V}{m\left(\dfrac{1}{2}d\right)} = \dfrac{qV}{md}$, therefore, **no change**.

5. *Three charges A, B, and C with charges respectively of +3.2 x 10^{-6} C, +4.4$10^{-6}$ C, and -7.8 x 10^{-6} C are placed as seen in the diagram. What is the force on B because of A and C ?*

Answer:

$$F_{\text{B by A}} = \frac{kq_1q_2}{R^2}$$

$$= \frac{(8.99 \times 10^9 \, \text{N m}^2/\text{C}^2)(3.2 \times 10^{-6}\text{C})(4.4 \times 10^{-6}\text{C})}{(2.5 \, \text{m})^2}$$

$$= 20.3 \times 10^{-3} \, \text{N} = 2.0 \times 10^{-2} \, \text{N}$$

$$F_{\text{B by C}} = \frac{kq_1q_2}{R^2}$$

$$= \frac{(8.99 \times 10^9 \, \text{N m}^2/\text{C}^2)(4.4 \times 10^{-6}\text{C})(7.8 \times 10^{-6}\text{C})}{(1.5 \, \text{m})^2}$$

$$= 137 \times 10^{-3} \, \text{N} = \mathbf{1.37 \times 10^{-1} \, N}$$

B experiences a push away from A, and attraction to C.

Therefore,   by vector diagram

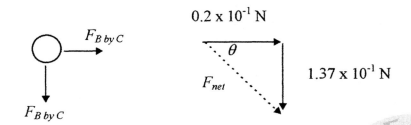

0.2 x 10^{-1} N

1.37 x 10^{-1} N

Therefore, $\boldsymbol{F_{net}}$ **= 1.38 x 10^{-1} N at** θ**= 81.7°**

6. *A radar set operates on 24 V and draws a current of 12 Amperes. How much energy does it use in a 24 hour period ?*

Answer: $E = Pt$

$\quad = VIt = (24\ V)(12\ A)(60\ min/hr)(60\ s/min)$

$\quad = \mathbf{2.5 \times 10^7\ J}$

7. *If the cost of the energy is $0.03 per kJ, what is the cost of operating the radar set in question 6 for 24 hours ?*

Answer: $2.5 \times 10^7\ J = 2.5 \times 10^4\ kJ$

Since $\dfrac{1\ kJ}{2.5 \times 10^4\ kJ} = \dfrac{\$0.03}{x}$

$\quad x = \mathbf{\$750.00}$

8. *Two conducting spheres with charges of +3.2 x 10^{-6} C and -4.8 x 10^{-6} C are touched together and then separated by a distance of 3.4 m. What is the magnitude of the force acting on each charge ?*

Answer: When touched , the two spheres share the net charge,

$q_{net} = -1.6 \times 10^{-6}\ C,$

and each charge has a charge $= q/2 = (-1.6 \times 10^{-6}\ C)/2$

$= -0.8 \times 10^{-6}\ C = -8.0 \times 10^{-7}\ C$

To determine the force acting between the two charges, use Coulomb's law

$$F_e = \frac{kq_1q_2}{R^2}$$

$$= \frac{(8.99 \times 10^9\ N\,m^2/C^2)(8 \times 10^{-7}\ C)(8 \times 10^{-7}\ C)}{(3.4\ m)^2}$$

$$= 49.8 \times 10^{-5}\ N = \mathbf{4.98 \times 10^{-4}\ N}$$

This force will be a force of repulsion, because each charge is

a negatively charged object.

9. a) *Find the total resistance of the circuit.*

b) *Find the current through each resistor.*

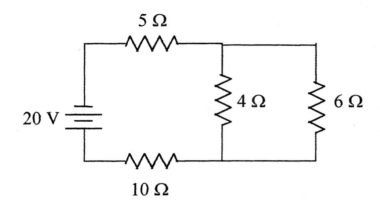

$$\frac{1}{R_p} = \frac{1}{4\,\Omega} + \frac{1}{6\,\Omega}$$

$$= \frac{6}{24} + \frac{4}{24} = \frac{10}{24}$$

$$R_p = 24/10 = 2.4\ \Omega$$

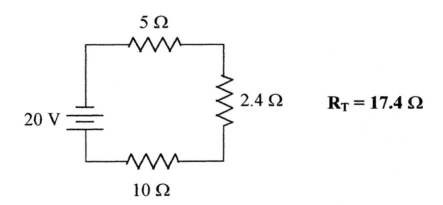

$$R_T = 17.4\ \Omega$$

Therefore, $I = \dfrac{V}{R} = \dfrac{20\ V}{17.4\ \Omega} = \mathbf{1.15\ A}$

This will be the current through 5 Ω and 10 Ω resistors.

Potential drop at 5 Ω resistor = IR = (1.15 A)(5 Ω)= 5.75 V

Potential drop at 10 Ω resistor = IR = (1.15 A)(10 Ω)= 11.5 V

Therefore,

the potential drop across 4 Ω resistor = 20V - (5.75 V+11.5 V)

$$= 2.75\ V$$

---

and $\quad I = \dfrac{V}{R} = \dfrac{2.75\ V}{4\ \Omega} = \textbf{0.69 A}$

Therefore,

the current through 2 Ω resistors = 1.15 A - 0.69 A = **0.46 A**

10. *It requires an average force of 6.00 x 10^{-3} N to move a 3.3 x 10^{-3} C charge from one point in an electric field to another point that is 1.2 m away. What is the potential difference between the two points ?*

Answer: $\quad V = \dfrac{work}{charge} = \dfrac{F_e d}{q} = \dfrac{(6.00 \times 10^{-3}\ N)(1.2\ m)}{3.3 \times 10^{-3}\ C} = \textbf{2.2 V}$

11. *On planet X, with mass 6.4 x 10^{34} kg, a 30 kg skwib weighs 742 N. What is the radius of the planet ?*

Answer: $\quad F_g = \dfrac{Gm}{R^2}$

therefore $\quad R^2 = \dfrac{Gm}{F_g}$

and $\quad R = \sqrt{\dfrac{Gm}{F_g}} = \sqrt{\dfrac{(6.67 \times 10^{-11}\ Nm^2/kg^2)(6.4 \times 10^{34}\ kg)}{742\ N}}$

$\sqrt{0.058 \times 10^{23}}\ N = \sqrt{58 \times 10^{20}}\ N = \textbf{7.6 x 10}^{10}\ \textbf{m}$

12. *A proton accelerates through a distance of 5.0 cm in an electric field of intensity 4.4 x 10¹ N/C. What will its final speed be, if it starts from rest ?*

Answer: The proton (q) experiences $F_e = q|E| = ma$

$$a = \frac{q|E|}{m} = \frac{(1.6 \times 10^{-19}\ C)(4.4 \times 10^1\ N/C)}{(1.67 \times 10^{-27}\ kg)} = 4.22 \times 10^9\ m/s^2$$

Now $v_f^2 = v_f^2 + 2ad$

$$= 0 + 2(4.22 \times 10^9\ m/s^2)(0.05\ m)$$

$$= 0.422 \times 10^9\ m^2/s^2$$

$$= 4.22 \times 10^8\ m^2/s^2$$

$$v_f = \sqrt{4.22 \times 10^8\ m^2/s^2}$$

$$= 2.05 \times 10^4\ m/s$$

$$= \mathbf{2.1 \times 10^4\ m/s}$$

or

Proton has work done on it $W = F_e\ d$

$$= q|E|d$$

This work will go to increase the KE of the proton, that is,

$$W = KE_{gain}$$

$$F_e\ d = \frac{1}{2} mv^2$$

$$q|E|d = \frac{1}{2} mv^2$$

$$v = \sqrt{\frac{2q|E|d}{m}}$$

---

13. *A charged oil drop has a mass of 3.6 x 10⁻¹² kg, and it is suspended in an electric field of intensity 3.5 x 10⁴ N/C. What is the charge in the oil drop ?*

Answer: Millikan's oil drop experiment

$$F_e = F_g$$

$$q|E| = mg$$

$$q = \frac{mg}{|E|} = \frac{(3.6 \times 10^{-12}\,kg)(9.81\,N/kg)}{3.5 \times 10^4\,N/C}$$

$$= 10.1 \times 10^{-16}\,C$$

$$\mathbf{= 1.0 \times 10^{-15}\,C}$$

14. *What is the number of electrons needed to give the oil drop in question 13 the charge you calculated ?*

Answer: # electrons $= \dfrac{charge}{charge/e} = \dfrac{1.0 \times 10^{-15}\,C}{1.6 \times 10^{-19}\,C/e} = 0.625 \times 10^4\,e$

$$\mathbf{= 6.25 \times 10^3\,e}$$

PHYSICS GRADE 12

Magnetic Fields and Electromagnetic Radiation

Magnetic Forces and Fields

If you are familiar with magnets, then you know that they attract pieces of iron, coins (like nickels), bits of metal. You may also know that magnets have two separate regions of attraction. These are called the **poles** of the magnet. One pole is the **North pole**, and is generally stamped with an N; the other is a **South pole**, and is stamped with an S. If a magnet is suspended from a string, so that it is free to swivel, it will align itself in a North-South direction with the North pole pointing to the North. This pole is often called the **North-seeking pole**. The other pole, the South pole, seeks the South.

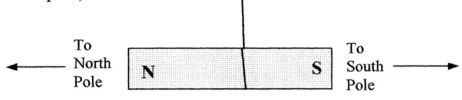

If two magnets come near each other, a magnetic force (F_m) will act between them. If the two near poles are *alike*, the force will be a force of repulsion. If they are *unlike*, it will be a force of attraction. We explain this force as an interaction caused by **magnetic fields**, the regions of influence that surround the magnets. A compass can be used to find the direction of the **lines of force** that surround a bar magnet.

A compass can be represented like this

A compass is a suspended magnet, and it will

align itself along a line of force when it is in a magnetic field. The north

pole of the compass would point towards the South pole of the magnet

creating the field. Placed at many points around the magnet, the lines of

force can be determined. Also placing a sheet of paper over a bar magnet,

and sprinkling iron filings on the paper will produce the same pattern.

The magnetic field surrounding a bar magnet can be represented like this:

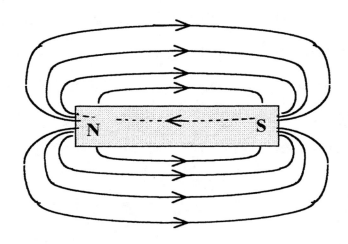

A magnet placed anywhere in this field will align itself along these lines

of force. We use a compass to give the field lines a direction. **The**

direction of a magnetic field at any point is the direction of the

magnetic force that acts on a North pole of a magnet that is placed at

that point in the field. You will notice the field lines are all directed

from the North pole   of the magnet to the South pole of the magnet.

The magnetic field lines, however, are continuous loops that pass from

South to North inside the magnet. Therefore, if a magnet is broken in

half, it will produce two new magnets, each with a North and South pole.

Law of Magnets

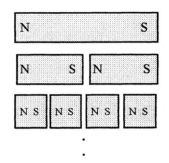

Unlike poles attract.

Like poles repel.

To atoms, which are
themselves small magnets

Magnets act differently than electrically charged objects.

Magnets	Charged Objects
• occur naturally as the mineral magnetite	• objects must be rubbed to become charged
• only metals exhibit magnetism	• any object can be electrically charged
• attract pieces of metal	• attract pieces of grass, paper, etc.
• two pole or regions of attraction: North and South	• one centre of attraction: + *or* -

Forces of attraction or repulsion caused by the interaction of the magnetic fields of the two magnets can be represented like this.

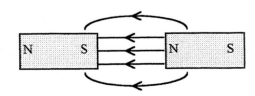

Attraction: field lines **pull** together

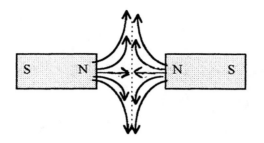

Repulsion: field lines **push** apart

In 1600 AD, Sir William Gilbert showed that the Earth is surrounded by a magnetic field. It is this field that affects compasses and causes them to point in a N-S direction. The field would resemble that of a bar magnet.

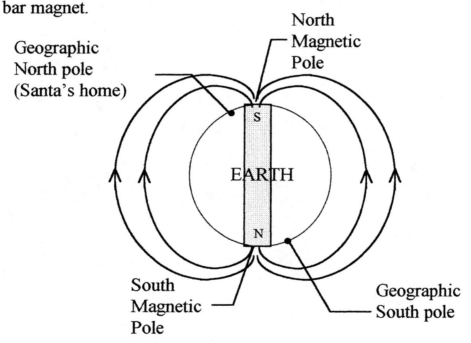

Since a compass placed in this field will have its North pole pushed towards Earth's North pole, the direction of the field lines is from Earth's South Magnetic pole to Earth's North Magnetic pole. Since for bar magnets, the direction of the magnetic field lines is always from the North pole to the South Pole, then **Earth's South magnetic pole** is really the North pole of a

PHYSICS GRADE 12

Magnetic pole to Earth's North Magnetic pole. Since for bar magnets, the direction of the magnetic field lines is always from the North pole to the South Pole, then **Earth's South magnetic pole** is really the North pole of a bar magnet, and the Earth's North magnetic pole is really the *South* pole of a magnet! Earth's field is rather weak (10^{-5} Tesla), and over thousands of years, it fluctuates in strength. Also, about every 80,000 years, the polarity changes (North pole becomes the South pole, and vice-versa). The source of Earth's magnetic field, the fluctuations, and polarity reversals is to this day a mystery!

In 1820, Hans Oerstead discovered that electricity could be used to produce a magnetic field. He found that a *current carrying conductor surrounds itself with a circular magnetic field* (B).

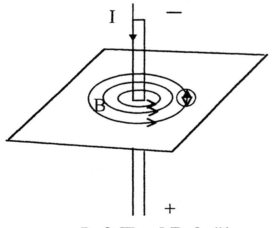

Left Hand Rule #1

The magnetic field that surrounds such a conductor is circular loops perpendicular to the conductor.

A left hand rule is used to determine the direction of the magnetic field around such a conductor. Point the left thumb in the direction of the electron flow, and your fingers of the left hand will curl around the conductor in the direction of the magnetic field. If the current stops, the magnetic field will disappear.

Andre Ampere showed, in 1821, that if two parallel conductors are each carrying a current, then a magnetic force of attraction or repulsion will

---

act between them. In other words, a current can exert a force on a current.

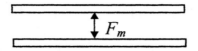

To know if the force is a force of attraction or repulsion, imagine two conductors running into the plane of this paper.

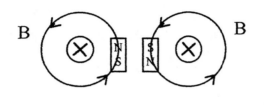

⊗ current into paper
⊙ current out of paper

You can see that the two magnets placed along the magnetic line of force circling this conductor have aligned themselves so the *North* points in the direction of the field. Because these two magnets would attract each other, so do the fields.

Therefore, if current is in the same direction through parallel conductors, a magnetic force of *attraction* will act on each conductor.

if

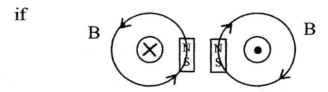

the magnets would repel.

Ampere used this idea to define the **Ampere of electric current**. "If the force that acts on each meter of two straight parallel conductors separated by 1 meter each is exactly 2×10^{-7} N, then the current in each conductor is exactly one Ampere."

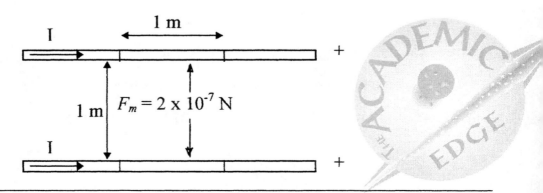

This force is a direct result of the electric current.

It is possible to use the magnetic field around a conductor to make an electromagnet.

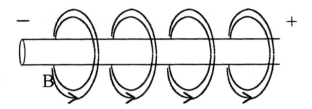

If this straight conductor was bent into a loop,

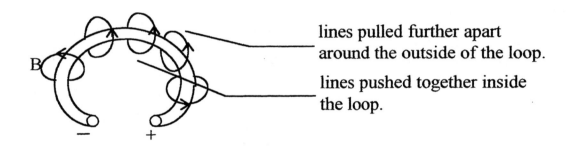

lines pulled further apart around the outside of the loop.

lines pushed together inside the loop.

The magnetic field is always strongest where the lines are closest together. If the loop was lying on the plane of the paper, the magnetic field inside the loop would be pointing up out of the paper.

If a conductor is wound into a coil, the magnetic fields of each loop unite to produce a strong magnetic field in the core of the coil.

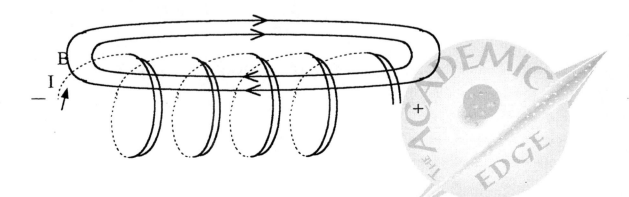

Imagine partially under the paper you are reading, and partly out of the paper, then the magnetic field in the plane of the paper would resemble that of a bar magnet. The magnetic field, B, is partly shown in the above diagram. If a **ferromagnetic** material (has good magnetic properties, like iron, nickel, or cobalt) is placed into the core, the magnetic field becomes even stronger.

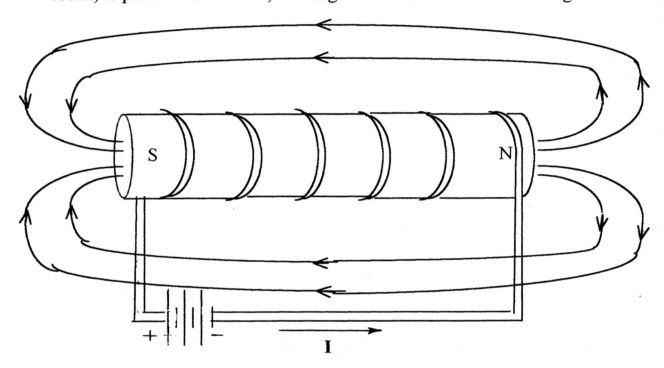

This makes what is called an **electromagnet**. The strength of the magnet depends upon,

> 1- the current: greater I means stronger electromagnet.
>
> 2- number of winds of conductor: greater number means stronger electromagnet.
>
> 3- core material: some are better than others.
>
> 4- core diameter: Smaller diameter means stronger electromagnet.

We can use another **left-hand rule** to determine the direction of the North pole of the electromagnet. This is rule is: "Curl the fingers of your left hand around the core in the direction of the electron flow, the current, - to +, and the thumb of your left hand will point in the direction of the North pole."

Electromagnets have many applications today as magnetic lifters, in speakers, cellphones, microphones, switches, and many other devices.

Now, the magnetic field that surrounds a conductor is only there when a current exists in the conductor. No current, no magnetic field. But you know that we do not need a conductor to have a current. A current is moving electric charges. Therefore, whenever an electric charge moves, it is a current and it surrounds itself with a circular magnetic field. An electric charge that is stationary is surrounded only by an electric field, but moving, it has an additional magnetic field.

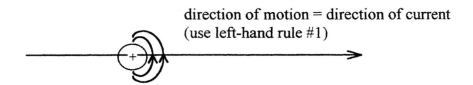

direction of motion = direction of current
(use left-hand rule #1)

Therefore, if a moving electric charge enter a magnetic field **perpendicular** to the magnetic field lines, it will experience a magnetic push which will be able to deflect it from its course. To study such a force, we use a uniform magnetic field, one where the strength is equal at all points. Such a magnetic field can be produced by bending a bar magnet, or using an electromagnet as seen below.

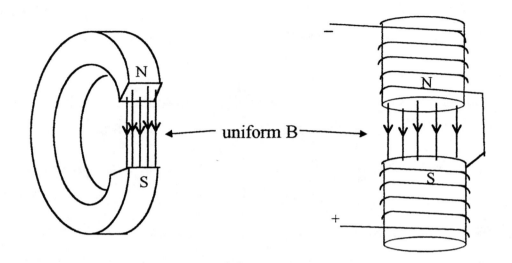

If we have such a uniform magnetic field in the plane of this page, and a charge moves in the plane of the page, perpendicular to B, than a deflecting force, F_m , will deflect the charge. If the charge is *negative*, use the *left* hand to determine the direction of F_m . If the charge is *positive*, use the *right* hand.

1.

2.

In 1, when q enters B, it will be deflected up out of the paper

In 2, when q enters B, it will experience a deflection down into the paper.

The **left hand rule #3** (right hand rule for +charges) goes like this. Point the fingers of the left hand in the direction of the magnetic field lines (always from North to South). Point the thumb of the left hand in the direction of the motion of the charge (usually perpendicular to B). Then the magnetic force that acts on q is in the direction that the *palm* of the left hand faces.

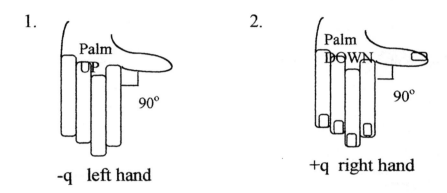

Note: The palm direction is perpendicular to both the fingers and the thumb. Stand your pencil up on the palm to see this perpendicular direction.

If the magnetic field was directed from left to right, and a negative charge moved through it into the paper, then you can see the magnetic interaction of the fields.

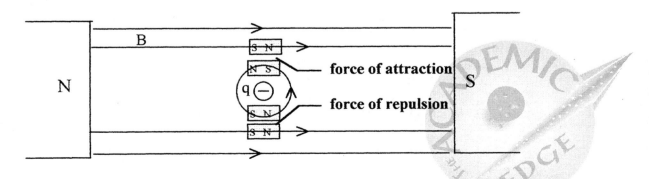

Negative charge moving into the paper (therefore we use left hand rule #1 to determine the direction of B around the moving charge; the current). Then point the fingers of your left hand from North to South in the direction of the magnetic field through which q will move. Rotate hand, keeping fingers pointing N to S until thumb points into the paper. Then *palm* faces the top of the page which is the direction of F_m on q, therefore q is deflected upwards.

If the magnetic field is in the plane of the page, so that if you can imagine a North pole above your paper, and a South pole beneath, then the magnetic field lines could be into the paper.

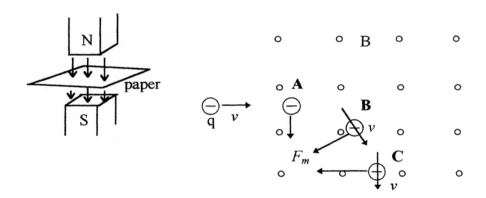

when **q** gets to A, it experiences F_m perpendicular to v and B (use left hand rule). Because direction is altered, q is deflected downwards. At position B, it has a velocity vector in a new direction, so (using left hand rule) note that F_m (still perpendicular to v and B) is in a new direction directed towards the center of the circle. Therefore F_m causes q to move in an arc through B, since F_m is a centripetal force.

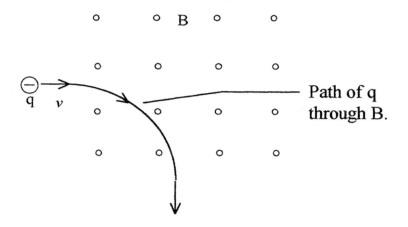

Path of q through B.

For F_m to act on q, there are some necessary conditions. q must be moving perpendicular to B, or at least have some component of its velocity perpendicular to B. If q has a velocity parallel to B, no magnetic force is present. If the field is strong, the field may trap the charge, keeping it moving in a circular path. The amount of force, F_m acting on the charge q moving at v through a magnetic field B is given by

$$F_m = qv_{\perp} B$$

where F_m = magnetic force acting on q, and *always* perpendicular to the direction of v (measured in Newtons).

q = charge of moving object (measured in Coulombs).

$v_{\perp}$ = velocity of charge perpendicular to B (measured in m/s).

B = magnetic field intensity (measured in Teslas, T).

If v is not parallel to B, then use v_x, which is perpendicular to B.

But $v_x = v \sin\theta$

therefore $F_m = qvB\sin\theta$

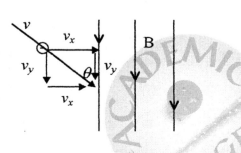

Since F_m is a centripetal force, we can know the radius of the arc through which q moves.

Since $\qquad F_m = F_c$

$$qvB = mv^2/R$$

and since v is the same on both sides of the equation,

$$R = \frac{mv}{qB},$$

where $\qquad m$ = mass of the object (kg)

v = speed of the object (m/s)

q = charge of the object (C)

B = magnetic field strength (T)

R = radius of object's path because of F_m (m)

The magnetic field strength or intensity is measured in Teslas.

$$1\,T = 1\,\frac{N}{A \cdot m} = 1\,\frac{Newton}{Amp \cdot meter} \quad or \quad 1\,\frac{N}{\frac{C}{s} \cdot m} = 1\frac{N \cdot s}{C \cdot m}$$

If a conductor is in a magnetic field, it can experience magnetic force, if a current exists in the conductor. Imagine B *into* the paper once again

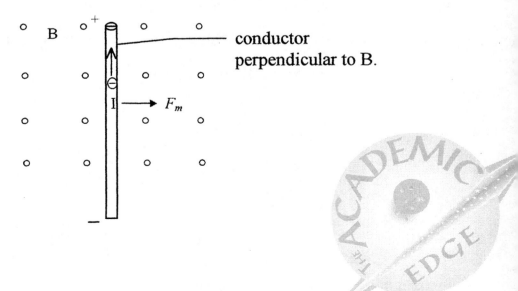

3. *If electrons are accelerated across a potential difference of 3.20 x 10² V, and the radius of their orbit in a magnetic field is 0.256 m, then what is the intensity of that magnetic field ?*

Answer: The electrons gain a KE of qV, which we can use to find v.

since $\quad KE = qV$

$$\frac{1}{2}mv^2 = qV$$

and $\quad mv^2 = 2qV$

so $\quad v = \sqrt{\frac{2qV}{m}} = \sqrt{\frac{2(1.6 \times 10^{-19}\,C)(3.20 \times 10^2\,V)}{(9.11 \times 10^{-31}\,kg)}}$

$$= 1.06 \times 10^7\,m/s$$

Now since

$$F_m = F_c$$

$$qvB = mv^2/R$$

then $\quad B = \dfrac{mv}{qR} = \dfrac{(9.11 \times 10^{-31}\,kg)(1.06 \times 10^7\,m/s)}{(1.6 \times 10^{-19}\,C)(0.256\,m)}$

$$= 23.6 \times 10^{-5}\,T$$

$$= \mathbf{2.36 \times 10^{-4}\,T}$$

4. An electron moves through a magnetic field of intensity 1.2 x 10⁻¹ T at a speed of 4.2 x 10⁶ m/s perpendicular to the field. What will the rate of acceleration of this charge be in the field ?

Answer: The electron will experience a magnetic force, F_m , perpendicular to the direction of its motion $F_m = qvB$. Since this is the net force acting on the electron, it will be responsible for the centripetal acceleration that the electron will experience. Therefore

$$F_m = F_{net}$$

$$qv_\perp B = ma$$

$$a = \frac{qv_\perp B}{m}$$

$$= \frac{(1.6 \times 10^{-19}\,C)(4.2 \times 10^6\,m/s)(1.2 \times 10^{-1}\,T)}{(9.11 \times 10^{-31}\,kg)}$$

$$= 0.885 \times 10^{17}\,m/s^2$$

$$= \mathbf{8.85 \times 10^{16}\ m/s^2}$$

This acceleration will be directed towards the centre of its circular path.

5. The period of an electromagnetic wave is 1.5 x 10⁻¹⁵ s. What is the wavelength of this radiation ?

Answer: Since $\lambda = \dfrac{c}{f}$ but $f = \dfrac{1}{T}$

therefore $\lambda = \dfrac{c}{\dfrac{1}{T}} = cT = (3.00 \times 10^8\,\dfrac{m}{s})(1.5 \times 10^{-15}\,s)$

$$= \mathbf{4.5 \times 10^{-7}\ m}$$

6. *An alpha particle and electron enter, at the same speeds and from the same direction, a strong magnetic field that curls them in opposite directions. How does the radius of the path of the α-particle compare to that for the electron ?*

Answer: We know that both will experience the sideways push, F_m, that depends upon $q v_\perp B$ for each particle. Since this force is a centripetal force,

$$F_m = F_c$$

$$qvB = mv^2/R$$

and

$$R = \frac{mv}{qB}$$

if

$$R_\alpha = \frac{m_\alpha v}{q_\alpha B} \quad \text{and} \quad R_e = \frac{m_e v}{q_e B}$$

then

$$\frac{R_\alpha}{R_e} = \frac{\dfrac{m_\alpha v}{q_\alpha B}}{\dfrac{m_e v}{q_e B}}, \text{ since } v \text{ and B are equal for both particles.}$$

$$\frac{R_\alpha}{R_e} = \frac{m_\alpha}{q_\alpha} \cdot \frac{q_e}{m_e} = \frac{m_\alpha (-1e)}{m_e (+2e)}, \text{ since } q_\alpha = q_e$$

$$= \frac{6.65 \times 10^{-27} \text{ kg}}{2(9.11 \times 10^{-31} \text{ kg})} = 0.365 \times 10^4$$

$$= 3.65 \times 10^3$$

Therefore, $\mathbf{R_\alpha = 3.65 \times 10^3 (R_e)}$. The radius of the α-particle's path is 3.65×10^3 times larger than the radius of the electron's path.

PHYSICS GRADE 12

Magnetic Fields and Electromagnetic Radiation
Practice Problems

1. Use the formula for $F_m = q\,v_\perp B$ to determine the units of a Tesla, the units used for measuring magnetic field strength.

2. An electron gun has an accelerating voltage of 4.80×10^2 Volts. The accelerated electrons then enter a magnetic field of intensity 4.00×10^{-5} T. What is the speed of the electrons as they enter the magnetic field, if their radius of curvature is 1.64 m ?

3. A proton enters a magnetic field in the same direction as the field at a speed of 3.8 x 10^6 m/s. If the magnetic field intensity is 1.5 x 10^{-3} T, then what is the amount of magnetic force acting on the proton ?

4

A $\bigcirc$ —→ v_A

B $\bigcirc$ —→ v_B

C $\bigcirc$ —→ v_C

magnetic field directed into the page

Describe the nature of each

particle.

5. A horizontal copper conductor with a length of 30.0 cm is placed perpendicular to Earth's magnetic field. The diameter of the conductor is 2 mm, and the density of copper is 8.92 g/cm^2.

What current is needed in the conductor to balance the gravitational forces on the conductor, and have the conductor suspended ?

6. An alpha-particle is accelerated and given a kinetic energy of

8.40×10^2 eV, and then is sent through a magnetic field at right angles to the field.

a) What is the speed of the alpha-particle ?

b) What magnetic field intensity is required to cause the alpha-particle to travel in a circular path of radius = 10 cm ?

7. A radio wave passes through 16 cm of air and then 12 cm of water, where it strikes a reflecting surface, and returns to the transmitter. What is the time required for the wave to complete the round trip ?

8. The time required for 2 wavelengths of an EM wave to pass a given point in space is 3.6×10^{-6} s. What is the wavelength of the wave ?

9. An ion with a charge of 2e in a magnetic field moves in a circle with radius=2.65 m. If the speed of the particle is 4.2 x 10^4 m/s, then what is its mass ?

10. An EM wave with a wavelength of 5.8 x 10^{-14} m has what period ?

11. In a special experiment, an electron beam is passed through perpendicular electric and magnetic fields. If the electrons have a speed of 2.6 x 10^4 m/s, and the magnetic field is 2.5 x 10^{-4} T, then what is the strength needed for the electric field so that the electrons are undeflected ?

PHYSICS GRADE 12

Magnetic Fields and Electromagnetic Radiation Practice Problem Solutions

1. Use the formula for $F_m = q v_\perp B$ to determine the units of a Tesla, the units used for measuring magnetic field strength.

Answer: Since $\qquad$ $F_m = q v_\perp B$, then

$$B = \frac{F_m}{q v_\perp} \quad \text{units of which will be} \quad \frac{N}{C \cdot \dfrac{m}{s}}$$

$$\therefore\ 1\,\text{T(measure of B)} = 1 \frac{N}{C \cdot \dfrac{m}{s}} \text{ or } 1 \frac{N}{\dfrac{C}{s} \cdot m} = 1 \frac{N}{A \cdot m}$$

2. An electron gun has an accelerating voltage of 4.80×10^2 Volts. The accelerated electrons then enter a magnetic field of intensity 4.00×10^{-5} T. What is the speed of the electrons as they enter the magnetic field, if their radius of curvature is 1.64 m ?

Answer: $\qquad$ $F_m = F_c$

$$qvB = \frac{mv^2}{R}$$

$$v = \frac{qBR}{m} = \frac{(1.6 \times 10^{-19}\,\text{C})(4.00 \times 10^{-5}\,\text{T})(1.64\,\text{m})}{9.11 \times 10^{-31}\,\text{kg}}$$

$$= 10.5 \times 10^7 \text{ m/s} = \mathbf{1.05 \times 10^8 \text{ m/s}}$$

3. *A proton enters a magnetic field in the same direction as the field at a speed of 3.8 x 10^6 m/s. If the magnetic field intensity is 1.5 x 10^{-3} T, then what is the amount of magnetic force acting on the proton ?*

Answer: $F_m = 0$, since proton (q) is travelling parallel to B.

4.

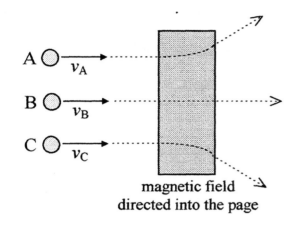

Describe the nature of each particle.

magnetic field
directed into the page

Use the left hand rule:

Particle A: Point fingers of righ hand in direction of B (into page), point thumb in direction of motion, then F_m acts towards top of page. Therefore, **particle A is positive**.

Particle B: No deflection by magnetic field, therefore no charge, **particle B is neutral**.

Particle C: Use left hand as in A. **Particle C is negative**.

5. A horizontal copper conductor with a length of 30.0 cm is placed perpendicular to Earth's magnetic field. The diameter of the conductor is 2 mm, and the density of copper is 8.92 g/cm². What current is needed in the conductor to balance the gravitational forces on the conductor, and have the conductor suspended?

Answer: Conductor must experience balanced forces to be suspended.

F_m will act up because F_g is down.

Therefore, $F_m = F_g = mg$

$IlB = mg$

so $I = \dfrac{mg}{l\,B}$

We need to know the mass. Use density and diameter.

Volume:

cross-sectional area $= \pi r^2$

$= \pi\,(1\text{ mm})^2$

$= \pi\,(10^{-3}\text{ m})^2$

$= 10^{-6}\,\pi\ \text{m}^2$

$= 3.14 \times 10^{-6}\text{ m}^2$

Volume = Area×length

$= (3.14 \times 10^{-6}\text{ m}^2)(0.3\text{ m})$

$= 0.94 \times 10^{-6}\text{ m}^3$

$= 9.4 \times 10^{-7}\text{ m}^3 \times 10^6\text{ cm}^3/\text{m}^3$

$= 9.4 \times 10^{-1}\text{ cm}^3$

Since density $= \dfrac{\text{mass}}{\text{volume}}$, then

mass $= D \times V$

$= (8.92\text{ g/cm}^3)(9.4 \times 10^{-1}\text{ cm}^3)$

$= 8.38\text{ g} = 8.38 \times 10^{-3}\text{ kg}$

Now,

$$I = \frac{mg}{l\,B} = \frac{(8.38 \times 10^{-3}\text{ kg})(9.81\text{ N/kg})}{(0.30\text{ m})(1.5 \times 10^{-5}\text{ T})}$$

$$= 182 \times 10^2\text{ A} = \mathbf{1.8 \times 10^4\,A}$$

6. *An alpha-particle is accelerated and give a kinetic energy of 8.40×10^2 eV, and then is sent through a magnetic field at right angles to the field.*

a) What is the speed of the alpha-particle ?

Answer: $\qquad KE = \dfrac{1}{2} mv^2$

Since $\qquad KE = 8.40 \times 10^2$ eV

$$= (8.40 \times 10^2 \text{ eV})(1.6 \times 10^{-19} \text{ J/eV})$$

$$= 13.44 \times 10^{-17} \text{ J} = 1.34 \times 10^{-16} \text{ J}$$

$$v = \sqrt{\frac{2KE}{m}} = \sqrt{\frac{2(1.34 \times 10^{-16} \text{ J})}{6.65 \times 10^{-27} \text{ kg}}} = \sqrt{0.40 \times 10^{11}} \text{ m/s}$$

$$= \sqrt{4.0 \times 10^{10}} \text{ m/s}$$

$$= \mathbf{2.0 \times 10^5 \text{ m/s}}$$

b) What magnetic field intensity is required to cause the alpha-particle to travel in a circular path of radius = 10 cm ?

Answer: $\qquad F_m = F_c$

$$qvB = \frac{mv^2}{R}$$

$$B = \frac{mv}{qR} = \frac{(1.67 \times 10^{-27} \text{ kg})(2.0 \times 10^5 \text{ m/s})}{(0.10 \text{ m})2(1.6 \times 10^{-19} \text{ C})}$$

$$= 10.4 \times 10^{-3} \text{ T}$$

$$= \mathbf{1.04 \times 10^{-2} \text{ T}}$$

7. *A radio wave passes through 16 cm of air and then 12 cm of water, where it strikes a reflecting surface, and returns to the transmitter. What is the time required for the wave to complete the round trip ?*

Answer: Since radio waves travel at c through air (3.00×10^8 m/s), then the time to travel through 16 cm of air and back again is

$$t = \frac{d}{v} = \frac{2(0.16 \text{ m})}{3.00 \times 10^8 \text{ m/s}} = \frac{0.32 \text{ m}}{3.00 \times 10^8 \text{ m/s}}$$

$$= 0.107 \times 10^{-8} \text{ s} = 1.07 \times 10^{-9} \text{ s}$$

Now, radio waves will travel slower through water

since $\qquad n = \dfrac{c}{v}$ (index of refraction)

$$v = \frac{3 \times 10^8 \text{ m/s}}{n} = \frac{3 \times 10^8 \text{ m/s}}{1.33} = 2.26 \times 10^8 \text{ m/s}$$

Therefore, the time to travel through 12 cm of H_2O and back at 2.26×10^8 m/s is

$$t = \frac{d}{v} = \frac{2(0.12 \text{ m})}{2.26 \times 10^8 \text{ m/s}} = \frac{0.24 \text{ m}}{2.26 \times 10^8 \text{ m/s}}$$

$$= 1.06 \times 10^{-9} \text{ s}$$

Therefore,

$$\text{total time} = t_{air} + t_{water} = 1.07 \times 10^{-9} \text{ s} + 1.06 \times 10^{-9} \text{ s}$$

$$= \mathbf{2.13 \times 10^{-9} \text{ s}}$$

PHYSICS GRADE 12

8. *The time required for 2 wavelengths of an EM wave to pass a given point in space is 3.6 x 10⁻⁶ s. What is the wavelength of the wave ?*

Answer: If two wavelengths require 3.6×10^{-6} s to pass a point in space,

then 1 wavelength requires 1/2 of that time $= 1.8 \times 10^{-6}$ s. This

is the period of the wave. Since EM waves travel at c,

then $\qquad v = f\lambda \qquad$ but $\qquad f = \dfrac{1}{T}$

so $\qquad v = \lambda \dfrac{1}{T} = \dfrac{\lambda}{T} \quad$ and $\quad \lambda = vT$

but $\qquad v = c$ for EM waves

therefore $\quad \lambda = cT = (3.00 \times 10^{8} \text{ m/s})(1.8 \times 10^{-6} \text{ s})$

$\qquad\qquad\qquad = \mathbf{5.4 \times 10^{2}}$ m (radio wave)

9. *An ion with a charge of 2e in a magnetic field moves in a circle with radius=2.65 m. If the speed of the particle is 4.2 x 10⁴ m/s, then what is its mass ?*

Answer:

$$F_m = F_c$$

$$qvB = \frac{mv^2}{R}$$

$$m = \frac{qBR}{v} = \frac{2(1.6 \times 10^{-19}\,\text{C})(4.3 \times 10^{-2}\,\text{T})(2.65\,\text{m})}{(4.2 \times 10^{4}\,\text{m/s})}$$

$$= \frac{36.46 \times 10^{-21}}{4.2 \times 10^{4}} = \mathbf{8.68 \times 10^{-17}\ kg}$$

10. *An EM wave with a wavelength of 5.8 x 10^{-14} m has what period ?*

Answer: $T = \dfrac{1}{f}$ but $f = \dfrac{c}{\lambda}$

therefore $T = \dfrac{1}{\dfrac{c}{\lambda}} = \dfrac{\lambda}{c} = \dfrac{(5.8 \times 10^{-7}\,\text{m})}{(3.0 \times 10^{8}\,\text{m/s})} = \mathbf{1.9 \times 10^{-15}\ s}$

11. *In a special experiment, an electron beam is passed through perpendicular electric and magnetic fields. If the electrons have a speed of 2.6 x 10^{4} m/s, and the magnetic field is 2.5 x 10^{-4} T, then what is the strength needed for the electric field so that the electrons are undeflected?*

Answer: $F_e = F_m$ (electric force must balance magnetic

force so no deflection)

$q|E| = qvB$

$|E| = (2.6 \times 10^{4}\ \text{m/s})(2.5 \times 10^{-4}\ \text{T}) = \mathbf{6.5\ N/C}$

PHYSICS GRADE 12

The Structure of Matter

After studying electricity and magnetism, we know that **light** is an **electromagnetic wave** that propagates through space at an incredibly fast rate (the speed of light), and stimulates our eyes to produce within us a sense of **sight**. In physics 20, we learn that light exhibits wave characteristics. It has a range of frequencies (about 10^{14} Hz) and wavelengths (10^{-7} m), refracts, travels through more optically dense materials like glass or water, diffracts (although slightly), interferes as observed by Thomas Young, may be polarized (indicating a **transverse** wave characteristic). Yet, light somehow remains mysteriously misunderstood as to its exact nature. Because light is produced by objects, a better understanding of **matter**, material that has mass and occupies space, may enhance our understanding of light. This section of physics 30 explores the atom by examining historically, discoveries made about atoms to convince the world of their existence, to know the structure of atoms, and finally to explain how atoms may emit light.

What is an Atom ?

The story of the atom begins with the ancient atomists of Greece (about 500 B.C.) who believed that if a person took a piece of matter, say a rock, and cut it in half, and then took a half a rock and cut it in half again, and continued to cut the rock into smaller and smaller

---

pieces, eventually, one would end up with a smallest piece of matter that could not be cut into smaller pieces. This smallest piece of matter was called an **atom**. The ancient atomists believed that all things are made of atoms. Their thoughts on atom produced these central ideas.

1- Atoms are eternal, they have always existed, and always will. Therefore, atoms cannot be created nor destroyed.

2- Atoms exist in a vacuum, hence because they exist in a vacuum with nothing between them, once atoms start moving, there will be nothing to stop them.

3- Atoms are in a continual state of motion.

4- They cannot be seen, being much smaller than the smallest object that can be seen visually.

5- When atoms are packed tightly together, they produce a solid. When in a looser formation, liquids are formed. When atoms are far apart, then a gas is formed.

6- Atoms may come together to form new materials (**compounds**), and are responsible for changes that occur in the world.

These ideas had followings, but other theories also claimed to explain matter. Aristotle believed that matter could be infinitely divided, so no need for invisible atoms. No need for a vacuum between the atoms. He taught that all matter was made up of four basic elements, AIR, EARTH, FIRE, and WATER, and that all things in this world are a combination (in different proportions) of these four basic elements.

He further taught that by changing these proportions, one substance could be made into another-specifically lead into gold. For nearly 2000 years, the ideas of the atomists were put aside while Alchemists searched for the secret of "lead into gold".

The Alchemists did make many chemical discoveries, and by the 18th century, chemistry was a growing science. Improvements in measuring instruments, chemical techniques, and laboratory recording and processing techniques gave new insights into matter, and led to the discovery of many empirical (experimentally determined) laws of chemical combination. Antoine Lavoisier, in the late 1700's, defined an element as "the simplest type of matter; matter that cannot further be divided into a simpler substance". By 1800, elements like gold, silver, carbon, mercury, sulfur, and others were known. About 25 in all.

In 1808, **John Dalton** revived the theory of atoms in order to explain the laws of chemical combination. His theory of atoms has five major points;

1- All material things consist of indivisible, invisible particles called atoms.

2- The atoms of any one element are alike in every respect: size, colour, shape, but especially mass.

3- Atoms of different elements are different in every respect. Therefore, there are as many different kinds of atoms as there are elements.

4- Atoms of different elements may combine to form the many different compounds that exist in this world. The smallest portion of such a compound will contain a certain number of atoms of each element (Here Dalton describes molecules).

5- In chemical reactions, atoms will only be rearranged. New atoms will not be made, nor will atoms be destroyed.

Using these ideas, Dalton explained the laws of chemical combination.

1- **Law of Conservation of Mass**: In a chemical reaction, the mass of the reactants equals the mass of the products.

2- **Law of Definite Proportion**: The ratio of the mass of one element to another in a compound is always constant for that compound.

Example: When water is formed from H_2 gas and O_2 gas, water always forms in the ratio 8 g O: 1g H.

3- **Law of Multiple Proportions**: Sometimes the same two elements will form different compounds, like CO (carbon monoxide) and CO_2 (carbon dioxide). In a sample of each containing equal masses of C, the mass of oxygen from the two samples is in a simple ratio.

Example: in 7g CO - 3 g C and 4 g O

and   in 11g CO_2 - 3 g C and 8 g O,

therefore $\dfrac{\text{O in CO}_2}{\text{O in CO}} = \dfrac{8 \text{ g}}{4 \text{ g}} = \dfrac{2}{1}$.

Dalton used his theory to determine the relative atomic masses of the atoms of the known elements. He determined that hydrogen atoms were the lightest of al atoms. He assigned them a mass = 1 **atomic mass unit**. Then he determined carbon atoms were 12x more massive. Their mass, relative to a hydrogen atom, was 12 atomic mass units (**amu**). Oxygen atoms has masses 16x that of a hydrogen atom, therefore the mass of an oxygen atom = 16 amu. You see these numbers in the periodic table as atomic mass number A.

$$^A_Z X \qquad A = \text{atomic mass number} \qquad ^1_1 H \quad ^4_2 He \quad ^{12}_6 C$$

$$Z = \text{atomic number}$$

Dalton further used his modern atomic theory to determine the combining capacity of each element's atoms, that is, the number of atoms that each atom of a give element could combine with. Today, we know these numbers as **oxidation numbers**, or **valence**; O^{2-}, F^{1-}, or Mg^{2+}. For each of the known elements at the time of John Dalton, he began to accumulate numerical data. Melting points, boiling points, combining capacity, densities, heat capacity, hardness, relative mass, etc. Scientists looked for a method to organize this information. In 1872, Dmetri Mendeleev introduced the **periodic table of the elements**. In organizing the elements in order of increasing atomic mass, and placing elements with similar properties into the same vertical columns, Mendeleev gave scientists a tool for assisting in atomic combination analysis. By examining trends that occur in this table, it is possible to predict outcomes of chemical reactions. The periodic repeating of chemical properties lead scientists to believe that atoms had an internal structure that may vary only slightly from element to element in the periodic table. Mendeleev was also able to make astounding predictions about the properties of unknown elements.

Because of Dalton's successes, and Mendeleev's grouping of elements based upon Dalton's relative atomic mass, the belief in atoms grew immensely during the nineteenth century.

Dalton gives us a picture of an atom. We call this model of the atom the **Billiard Ball Model**. Imagine atoms as being like billiard balls. Solid, compact, interacting with one another to form compounds. In picture form

A "Dalton" atom.

Remember that Dalton believed these very tiny particles were indivisible, therefore this atom is featureless, as we know of nothing inside the atom. Yet other investigations by other scientists lead to new discoveries, and a deeper understanding of atoms.

After 1800, when Alessandro Volta discovered electric batteries, it was found that *electricity* could be used to decompose compounds into their basic elements quite easily. This process is called **electrolysis**. Electricity is somehow connected to atoms. Micheal Faraday showed that a certain amount of electricity is associated with each mass of an element liberated in an electrolysis apparatus. For example, he found that the charge-to-mass ration for hydrogen atoms was 9.65×10^7 C/kg.

Cathode Rays and Electrons

In 1885 Heinrich Geissler produced a good vacuum pump. His cousin, Julius Plucker connected an electrical source (battery) to a glass tube, from which the air is removed almost totally. When the gas in the tube was at very low pressure, an electric current existed in the tube, and the tube emitted light! These tubes are called **gas discharge tubes**. In 1875, the tubes were called **cathode ray tubes**, or **CRT**'s. Sir William Crooks did an extensive study of these rays. A CRT is constructed like this.

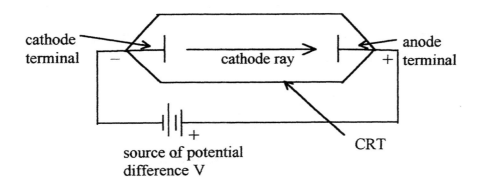

Crookes, by using various types of tubes, determined these properties for cathode rays.

    1- They are produced at the cathode terminal, and travel through the tube to the anode.

    2- They travel in straight lines perpendicular to the surface that emits them.

    3- They carry energy.

4- The cathode terminal can be made of any electrical conducting material, and rays with the same properties are produced.

5- A magnetic field can deflect these rays.

6- Cathode rays can expose photographic paper.

7- Crookes suspected, but was unable to prove that cathode rays could be deflected by an electric field.

These properties had scientists arguing for 25 years about the nature of these mysterious rays. Were cathode rays some form of light, or were they beams of very tiny electrically charged particles ? J. J. Thompson, in 1897 determined that they were in fact, charged particles. In a special cathode ray tube, Thompson showed that these rays were made of very small, negatively charged particle which he called **electrons**. His tube worked like this

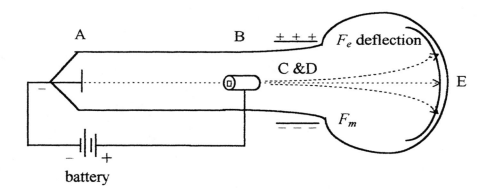

In this vacuum tube, A is the cathode. Electrons will be emitted from A. The anode is B. Electrons will travel from A to B inside the tube. Most will stick to the anode, and be returned to A by the battery. However, some will pass through the slit in the anode and form a single beam that will travel through C and D to a fluorescent screen at E. Now, at C and

D we introduce an electric field $|E|$ (between the two charged plates), and a magnetic field B perpendicular to $|E|$. Now if only $|E|$ is operating, then electrons are deflected upwards as they pass between the charged plates. This deflection is cause by the electrical force, F_e (remember $F_e = q|E|$). If $|E|$ is shut off, and only B (directed into the plane of the page) is in place, then the electrons are deflected downwards by a magnetic force, $F_m = qvB$. By using both fields set at the correct strength, F_e can be balanced by F_m, and the electrons can travel through both fields without being deflected.

That is $\qquad F_e = F_m$

$$q|E| = qvB$$

since q is the charge carried by each electron ($q = 1.6 \times 10^{-19}$ C), then the equation simplifies to

$$|E| = vB$$

and $\qquad\qquad v = $ the speed of the electrons

$$v = \frac{|E|}{B}$$

The speed of the electrons can be shown as the ratio of the two field strengths necessary to cause no deflection. The electrons emitted from the cathode terminal are given a velocity by being accelerated through the potential difference that exists between the cathode and the anode. Remember,

$$KE_{gain} = qV$$

For slow moving electrons, we can then find v by setting

$$qV = \frac{1}{2}mv^2$$

and solving for *v*. But when Thompson did the experiment, he had no idea of the charge or mass of the particles in a cathode ray beam. So, using the field ratios to determine *v*, the electric field is then turned off. The electrons in the cathode ray beam will then be deflected by the magnetic force. Because this force always acts perpendicular to the direction of the motion of the charges, the electrons move in an *arc* through the field. Such a force is, of course, a centripetal force, and

$$F_m = F_c$$
$$qvB = mv^2/R$$

v is the same on both sides of the equation, and solving for $\frac{q}{m} = \frac{v}{BR}$.

The charge-to-mass ratio for electrons can be determined. Thompson found that q/*m* for electrons was 1.76×10^{11} C/kg. He recalled that q/*m* for hydrogen atoms (ions) was 9.54×10^7 C/kg. In order for electrons to have a much larger q/*m* ratio, then either q was larger for electrons, or they had a much smaller mass than the smallest atom. He determined that one hydrogen atom ion carries a +charge, an electron a negative charge, and each had equal amounts of charge, as when they were combined, an electrically neutral atom of hydrogen was produced. Therefore, the masses of the particles must be much different. He determined that electrons are almost 1830 times less massive than hydrogen ions.

PHYSICS GRADE 12

The Charge of an Electron

In 1916, Robert Millikan, in his oil drop experiment, determined that the smallest unit of charge was 1.6×10^{-19} C, the charge of one electron. When this charge was determined, the mass of one electron could be known.

That is $\qquad q/m = 1.76 \times 10^{11}$ C/kg, but $q = 1.6 \times 10^{-19}$ C

Therefore $\quad m_e = \dfrac{q}{1.76 \times 10^{11} \dfrac{C}{kg}} = \dfrac{1.6 \times 10^{-19} \, C}{1.76 \times 10^{11} \dfrac{C}{kg}} \cong 9.11 \times 10^{-31}$ kg

Because a hydrogen ions is simply one proton, the mass of one proton could be known

$$1830 \times m_e = 1830 \times 9.11 \times 10^{-31} \text{ kg} = 1.67 \times 10^{-27} \text{ kg} = m_p$$

This is approximately the mass of one atomic mass unit. Now, from Dalton, the relative mass of atoms were known. Because oxygen atoms are 16x more massive than hydrogen atoms, scientists now know the mass of any atom in kg. That is, one oxygen atom has a mass $= 16 \times m_p$

$= 16 \times (1.67 \times 10^{-27} \text{ kg})$.

Thompson has show that electrons are common to all matter, and are part of all atoms. He adjusted our picture of what an atom is. He described atoms as consisting of matter that was mostly positive, but with enough electrons sprinkled throughout to make the atom electrically neutral.

Thompson's model of the atom is represented like this

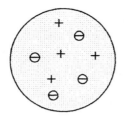

We call this model the Raisin Bun Model. The positive matter is like bread, and the electrons are like raisins sprinkled throughout.

In this model of "What is an atom ?", Thompson introduced the *electrical nature* of atoms. Note that

1- Equal amount of two types of electricity, + and -.

2- Most of the mass is associated with the positive matter.

3- The atom is *full* of + and - matter

4- Atoms have internal structure.

Thompson could not explain electron arrangement or number of electrons in an atom of a given element.

Proof of the existence of electrons was also provided by the **Photoelectric Effect**. Here electrons are obtained from matter by using light with a sufficiently high frequency.

The Photoelectric Effect

The photoelectric effect was first discovered by Heinrich Hertz in 1887. This is the same Hertz that showed experimentally the production and reception of electromagnetic waves as predicted by Maxwell's theory was, in fact, correct.

Hertz found that electrons could be produced when EM radiation (EMR) of frequency above some lowest frequency (called **the**

threshold frequency, f_o), would strike a material. These electrons are, in every respect, identical to the electrons produced in cathode ray tubes. In other words, there are two ways to produce a beam of electrons.

  1- cathode ray tube

  2- photoelectric effect.

Any material can exhibit this effect under the correct conditions.

To describe the photoelectric effect;

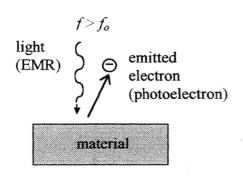

Light (EMR) of sufficiently high frequency strikes a material, and this energy is transferred to an electron which "pops" free of the surface. To show that these electrons are produced by using light, the electrons produced by this means are called **photoelectrons**.

Einstein explained the photoelectric effect using **quantum theory**. This effect cannot be explained using classical wave theory for light. According to classical theory, waves carry energy continuously.

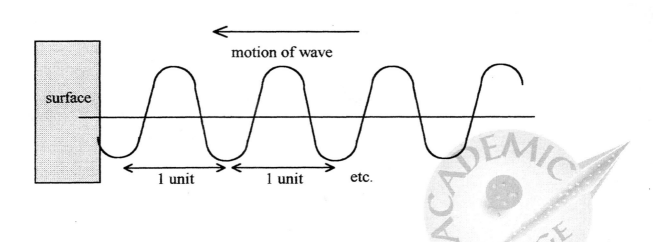

An electron near the surface can absorb any amount of energy from the incident light. If $f < f_o$, for an electron to absorb enough energy (to increase its own KE) it merely needs to wait for a long enough period of time. Yet, this does not happen. If $f < f_o$, no photoelectrons are emitted no matter how long we wait for energy from the light wave to be absorbed. But if $f > f_o$, photoelectrons are emitted immediately. It seems it takes no time for the energy to be absorbed by the electron. Classical theory cannot explain threshold frequency.

But according to Einstein, using an idea put forth by Max Planck, light carries its energy in **packages**. Each package is called a **quantum**, or today we call it a **photon**. If an electron is to absorb energy, it can absorb one photon, or 2 photons, or 3 photons etc. **A photon is the *smallest* amount of energy that can be obtained from light of a given frequency**. The energy in a photon is directly related to its frequency.

$E = hf$ E = energy of photon (1 package), in Joules.

h = **Planck's constant** = 6.63×10^{-34} Joule-seconds.

f = frequency of EMR.

Notes about the photoelectric effect.

1- If the frequency, f, of the incident light is below f_o, the threshold frequency for that material, no photoelectrons are emitted. Different substances have different threshold frequencies (most substances have a threshold frequency in the ultraviolet region of the EM spectrum).

2- A bright light (very intense beam) will produce no photoelectrons so long as f for the light is $< f_o$ for the material.

3- A very dim light (low intensity) can produce photoelectrons so long as f for the light is $> f_o$..

4- If $f > f_o$., then the brighter the light, the greater the number of photoelectrons emitted per unit of time (**photoelectric current**).

5- If $f > f_o$., then as f increases, so does the kinetic energy of the emitted photons.

6- To explain this effect, **quantum theory** must be used.

If $f > f_o$

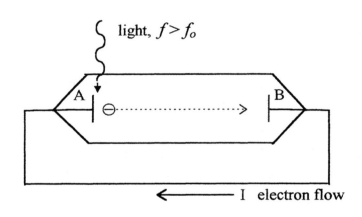

light, $f > f_o$

I   electron flow

As light strikes terminal A inside a vacuum tube, photoelectrons are knocked free. They travel to B. After some time, A is +charged and B is -charged unless we can allow the electron to move back to A by the external conductor. The light provides the energy to separate the positive and negative charge. This device is called a photoelectric cell. It converts light energy into electrical energy.

By using a battery in this circuit, we can study an interesting aspect of a photoelectron, its kinetic energy. The battery makes plate B

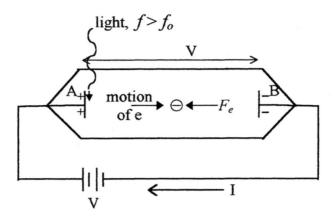

negative with respect to A. When light, $f > f_o$, strikes A, photoelectrons are emitted with a KE. They enter the electric field

between A and B, and experience F_e opposite to their direction of motion. If F_e is weak, photoelectrons reach B, and a current will exist in the circuit as shown. The strength of $|E|$ can be altered by adjusting the potential difference (batteries). $|E|$ may be strong enough to stop the most energetic photoelectrons from reaching B terminal. We can then use the potential difference between the plates to determine the maximum kinetic energy of emitted photoelectrons.

$$KE_{max} = q\, V_{stop}, \qquad q = \text{charge of electron.}$$

If an electron is struck by a photon, the photon will transfer its energy to the electron. The KE of the electron will increase. The electron must then lose some of this energy in doing some work to overcome the forces of attraction between + and -charges in matter. The electron would then have some energy left over for KE, so long as enough energy was supplied in the photon.

Einstein expresses this idea in a formula,

$$KE_{max} = hf - W$$

The maximum KE of an emitted electron = the energy absorbed from the incident photon - work to overcome force of attraction. If KE = 0, then

$$hf = W$$

and $\quad f = f_o$ for KE = 0,

therefore $\quad hf_o = W$

So Einstein's equation becomes

$$KE_{max} = hf - hf_o$$

(since no photoelectrons are emitted if $f < f_o$, it is understandable that $hf_o = W$)

Using this idea (energy in packages), threshold frequencies can be explained. Also, if we assume that one photon is absorbed by one electron, then,

light intensity $\propto$ number of photons in the light beam

number of photons $\propto$ number of photoelectrons emitted/unit

of time (photoelectric current)

therefore *light intensity $\propto$ photoelectric current*

That is, the brighter the light of $f > f_o$, the greater the current of electrons (photoelectrons) that will be produced. Experimental results agree with Einstein's claim.

In 1916, Robert Millikan showed that $KE_{max} \propto f$ of incident light. A linear relationship is demonstrated by substances A and B. A has a lower threshold frequency. A higher frequency is needed for substance B to initiate to emission of photoelectrons. But once started, KE increase as f increases.

If $f < f_o$, KE of photoelectrons is 0 or less (photoelectrons not emitted).

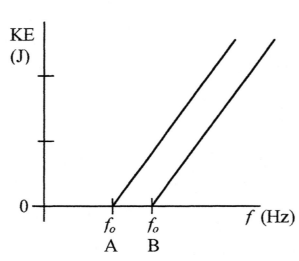

Einstein's explanation of this effect posed a problem for scientists. Light has wave properties when we examine how it diffracts, interferes, or can be polarized, but light behaves more like a particle in how it carries energy. This effect is good evidence to support a particle theory for light. Light carries its energy in packages.

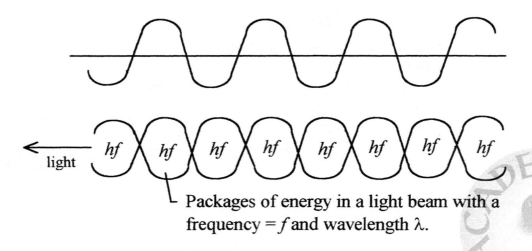

Packages of energy in a light beam with a frequency $= f$ and wavelength λ.

PHYSICS GRADE 12

X-Rays

About the same time as Einstein was explaining the photoelectric effect using quantum theory, and Thompson was discovering the electron, Wilhelm Röntgen (1895) discovered x-rays. They can be produced by a cathode ray tube.

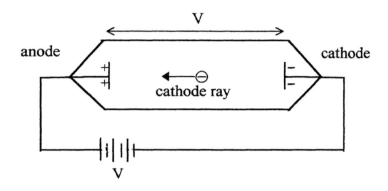

Electrons are accelerated across V from cathode to anode. They gain $KE = qV$. When the electron strikes the anode, the KE is carried away as a photon. The maximum frequency of the x-ray produced can be determined from $hf_{max} = qV$

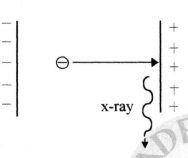

Röntgen determined that x-rays

    1- travel in straight lines

    2- expose photographic paper

    3- are *not* deflected by a magnetic field.

4- wave properties (diffraction) indicate a very short wavelength.

5- can be used to exhibit photoelectric effect with most materials.

6- have a high frequency that allows them to penetrate through solid materials (used immediately in medical research and diagnosis).

It seems that x-rays carry their energy in packages!

The Discovery of the Nucleus

Ernest Rutherford, in 1912 added the concept of a nucleus to atomic structure. He conducted a series of scattering experiments. He used alpha-particles (helium nuclei) emitted from a radioactive substance like bullets, and fired them through a very thin sheet of gold. Believing that gold atoms were constructed like Thompson's model, Rutherford believed the fast moving alpha-particles would easily pass through the much larger gold atoms, being deflected only slightly by chance encounters with electrons within the atoms.

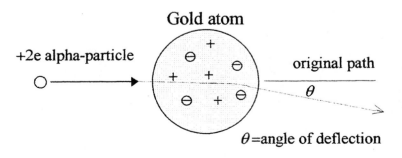

Gold atom

+2e alpha-particle

original path

θ

θ = angle of deflection

small angle of deflection caused by electric forces of attraction between + alpha-particle and negative electrons.

According to Rutherford, if atoms are constructed like Thompson describes, then the density of an atom (= mass/volume) would be very low. The fast moving, quite massive, alpha-particles should easily pass through the atom and not be deflected. Small angle deflection could be possible if α-particle pass near electrons inside the atoms of gold. The scattering experiments were conducted in a chamber like this.

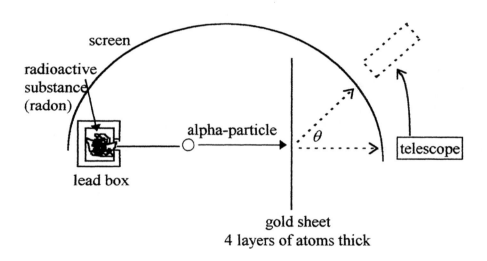

The screen was coated with a special material that emitted a small amount of light when struck by an alpha-particle. The telescope could be swiveled in an arc, so the numbers of alpha-particles deflected at given angles θ could be counted. After the experiment, Rutherford was very surprised to learn that some α-particles were actually deflected through angles of greater than 90°. These α-particles had stuck something very massive in the atom and bounced back. Because only one in 8000 was deflected through such a large angle, it seemed that it was unlikely that an α-particle would collide with the massive part of the atom, indicating the mass was small and occupied only a small region in each atom. Rutherford then gave this description of atoms to account for the scattering experimental results.

"An atom has most of its mass and all of its positive charge located in the centre of the atom (he called this the **nucleus**). Around this, the electrons are scattered in orbits like planets around the Sun."

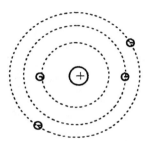

This model of the atom is called the **planetary model**.

With this model, Rutherford made some amazing claims.

1- The radius of the nucleus is about 1000× less than the radius of the atom. Therefore, the nucleus occupies only 1 *billionth* of the total volume of the atom.

2- Most of the atom is empty space in which electron may be found.

3- The charge carried by the nucleus could be determined. He found the number of positive elementary charges = atomic number.

$$_Z^A X$$

A = atomic mass number $\quad_1^1 H \qquad _2^4 He \qquad _6^{12} C$

Z = atomic number $\qquad$ +1 charge $\quad$ +2 charges $\quad$ +6 charges

Today we know that the atomic number = number of protons in the nucleus (remember that each proton has a charge equal to that of an electron, but where the electron's charge is negative electricity, the proton has positive electricity).

4- Number of electrons in each atom = atomic number, since the number of protons = number of electrons in a normal neutral atom to achieve 0 net charge.

5- Each element had atoms that have a fixed amount of +charge in the nucleus. In other words, all carbon atoms have 6 protons in their nucleus. If an atom has 7 protons, then it is a nitrogen atom. The proton count in the nucleus determines the type of atom, and gives the atom its chemical nature (All atoms with 6 protons will behave chemically as carbon atoms).

Rutherford's model incorporated Dalton's ideas of atoms and Thompson's ideas of electricity, plus could account for the observed scattering of α-particles. It was also able to show that the elements in the periodic table were arranged in order of proton count in the nucleus, but his model caused many questions about atoms.

1- Positive and negative charges are located in separate regions within an atom. What keeps the negative electrons from being pulled into the nucleus by electrostatic forces ?

2- How are the electrons arranged around the nucleus

3- What is the composition of the nucleus ? (protons alone could not account for all the mass)

4- What holds the nucleus together ? (with so many positive charges together, forces of repulsion should cause the nucleus to explode)

To answer some of these questions, Neils Bohr, in 1913, presented a more complex view of atoms. He was also interested in explaining the periodic chemical properties of the elements, and the unique line spectra emitted by hot gases.   His atomic theory is spectacular on these two counts.

The Hydrogen Spectrum

A gas can be "excited", so that it emits light in various ways. The gas can be heated, and when it is hot, it will emit light. When an electric current is passed through the gas in a vacuum tube containing a small amount of the gas, the gas in the tube will emit light. If the gas is that of an element like hydrogen, helium, sodium, or even mercury, the light emitted contains only certain frequencies, or colours. For example, helium gas emits an orange coloured light. This light is the combination of seven or eight separate frequencies. When the light is passed through a prism so that the light is dispersed into its individual colours, the spectrum so obtained is called a **bright-line spectrum** or **emission spectrum**. Hydrogen gas emits a pinkish-purple colour of light. When this light is separated into its colours , we find only four frequencies combine to form this light. The four frequencies contain a red, blue, and two violet frequencies. The bright line spectrum would look like this.

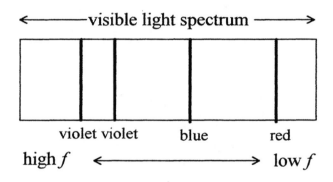

To distinguish between the lines, the lines are called the red, green, blue, and violet lines.

The wavelengths of these lines was known through experiments like Thomas Young's double slit experiment. Each element produced a unique spectrum of bright lines when, as a gas, it is excited. It seems that *an excited gas will emit only certain frequencies of light in the visible light region.* Hot solids and liquids produce **continuous spectra** (all frequencies). If light from a hot solid passes through a cool elemental gas, certain frequencies are absorbed by the gas. This removes certain colours from the continuous spectrum, leaving dark lines in the continuous spectrum. Such a spectrum is called a **dark line spectrum**, or an **absorption spectrum**. A gas, like hydrogen, will absorb those frequencies from the visible light region of the electromagnetic spectrum that it will emit when *it* is excited. It seems that a gas (of any given element) will emit only certain frequencies of visible light when it is excited, and will absorb those same frequencies when it is a cool gas.

Johann Balmer, in 1885 discovered an equation that could be used to determine the wavelength of the light emitted by excited hydrogen gas. The equation is in its modern form:

$$\frac{1}{\lambda} = R_H \left(\frac{1}{n_f^{\,2}} - \frac{1}{n_i^{\,2}} \right)$$

In this equation λ is the wavelength of a line in the spectrum of hydrogen gas.

R_H = Rydberg's constant for hydrogen = 1.1×10^7 /m.

n_f = 2

n_i = 3 for red line

= 4 for green line

= 5 for blue line

= 6 for violet line

The formula yields results that are in almost perfect agreement with experimental results.

The equation suggested that other lines, or wavelengths exist if n_i = 7, 8, 9 etc. The λ's calculated are λ's in the ultraviolet region. These lines were discovered to exist in the spectrum of hydrogen. We call this series of spectral lines the **Balmer series**.

If $n_f = 1$ $n_i = 2, 3, 4, ...$ λ's corresponding to another series of lines in the ultraviolet region of the electromagnetic spectrum called the **Lyman series**.

If $n_f = 3$ $n_i = 4, 5, 6, ...$ A series of infrared lines called the **Paschen series**.

If $n_f = 4$ $n_i = 5, 6, 7, ...$ A series of infrared lines called the **Brackett series**.

If $n_f = 5$ $n_i = 6, 7, 8, ...$ A series of infrared lines called the **Pfund series**.

These lines were discovered to exist in the spectrum of hydrogen gas light. In all there are five series of spectral lines. Each series contains an infinite number of lines. Pictorially, this can be represented as

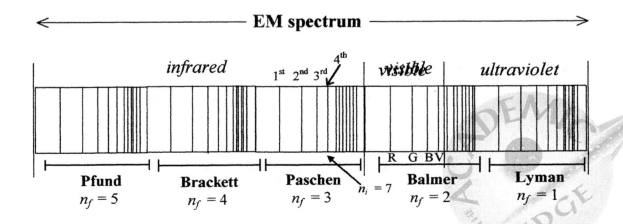

To determine the wavelength of any line in any series, set n_f = the numbers indicated above, then set $n_f = n_i$ + line number. So for example, if we wanted to know the wavelength of the 4th line in the Paschen series, use the equation

$$\frac{1}{\lambda} = R_H \left(\frac{1}{n_f{}^2} - \frac{1}{n_i{}^2} \right),$$

where $n_f = 3$, $n_i = 3 + 4 = 7$.

Why did this equation work so well ? Bohr explains this in 1913, with his atomic theory. Bohr's theory is based upon three **postulates**: statements *assumed to be true, without proof.*

Quantum Theory

Bohr believed that an atom was constructed like Ernest Rutherford suggested (planetary model), but Bohr realized that for electrons to exist at a distance away from the positive nucleus, the electrons had to be in orbits. The electric force of attraction would supply the centripetal force necessary to maintain circular orbits. But according to Maxwell's theory of electromagnetic radiation, an accelerating charge will initiate an EM wave that will carry energy away from the charge. An orbiting electron, theoretically, should lose energy and spiral into the nucleus, and the atom should collapse. Using a hydrogen atom as a simple example,

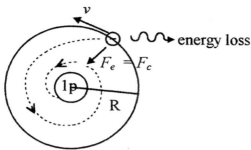

In theory, $F_e = F_c$ cause a centripetal acceleration ($a_c = \dfrac{v^2}{R}$), the electron emits EM radiation, loses energy, and moves into the nucleus.

Bohr's First Postulate: Since atoms don't collapse, there must be orbits which are allowed in which the electron, even though accelerating, will not emit EM radiation. These orbits are called **allowable orbits**, or **stationary states** of the atom.

In a picture, we represent the allowable orbits like this.

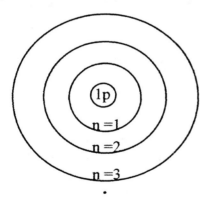

Each orbit is assigned a number called a **quantum number**. n = 1 is used to denote the first allowable orbit, n = 2 is the second allowable orbit, etc.

The first allowable orbit is the normal location for an electron in a hydrogen atom. If the electron is in the *first* allowable orbit, we say the atom is in its **unexcited state**, or the electron is in its **ground state**. If the atom absorbs energy, the electron will be in a higher numbered orbit.

It is possible to determine the radius of any allowable orbit

from $\boxed{r_n = n^2\, r_1}$

where

$r_1 = 5.29 \times 10^{-11}$ m (the radius of the first allowable orbit)

r_2 = radius of second allowable orbit

$\quad = 2^2\, r_1$

$\quad = 4(5.29 \times 10^{-11}\ \text{m}) = 2.17 \times 10^{-10}$ m

---

Bohr's Second Postulate: If a photon (quantum theory) strikes a hydrogen atom, the atom can absorb the energy and the electron will make a transition (move) to a higher numbered orbit. If the electron is in $n = 2$, or 3, or 4, etc., the atom is said to be "**excited**". If the electron is in $n = 1$, the atom is **unexcited**. An excited atom of hydrogen will become unexcited by then emitting a photon of light. So Bohr's second postulate states that when an atom absorbs or emits energy, electrons will make a transition from one allowable state to another.

In a picture:

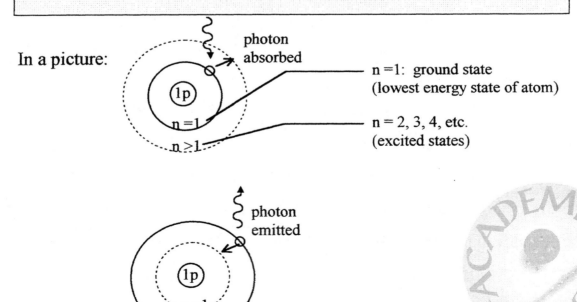

Since the energy absorbed or emitted is as photons, and the energy of a photon, $E = hf$, the frequency of the photon can be determined if we know the *difference in energy* of the electron when it moves from one allowable (energy) state to another. Algebraically, this is written as

$$hf = E = E_i - E_f$$

$$\text{where} \quad E_i = \text{energy in initial state}$$

$$E_f = \text{energy in final state}$$

The equation used to determine the energy in *any* state is given by

$$E_n = \frac{E_1}{n^2}$$

where $\quad E_1 = -13.6 \text{ eV}$

Therefore $\quad E_2 = \dfrac{E_1}{2^2} = \dfrac{E_1}{4} = \dfrac{-13.4 \text{ eV}}{4} = -3.4 \text{ eV}$

Now, the energy of a hydrogen atom is at its lowest amount when the electron is in $n = 1$. To have the electron move to $n = 2$, the atom must *absorb energy*. The difference in the two energy states, or allowable states is 10.2 eV. A photon carrying exactly this energy may be absorbed by the atom, and in doing so, the electron moves from $n = 1$ to $n = 2$.

$$-13.6 \text{ eV} + \quad E \quad = -3.4 \text{ eV}$$

$$n = 1 + \text{energy} \rightarrow n = 2$$

The energies are negative because the electron's energy is compared to that of a "free" electron; one so far removed from the nucleus (at $n = \infty$), that it is free of electrical forces of attraction. Such an electron has an assigned energy= 0 eV. Therefore, to move an electron in a hydrogen atom from n = 1 (innermost state) to a "free state", 13.6 eV must be added to the atom.

In a picture

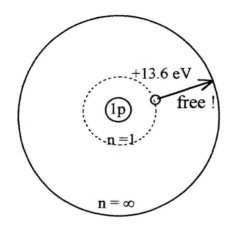

This is the energy necessary to **ionize** a hydrogen atom. i.e. "strip an electron from the atom , producing an H^+ ion."

Since there are unique energy differences between allowable orbits, only certain frequencies of light energy will be absorbed by the atom.

Once an atom is excited, the electron will, soon after, move "back down" to lower energy states, and the atom will emit photons of light. However, if a hydrogen atom is excited so that the electron is in the allowable orbit defined by n = 6, when the electron moves back down to

n = 1 (ground state) it can do so in many ways.

1. It can go from n = 6 to n = 1 in a single "jump" emitting one photon with an energy

$$E = E_6 - E_1$$

$$= \frac{E_1}{6^2} - E_1$$

$$= -0.38 \text{ eV} - (-13.6 \text{ eV})$$

$$= 13.2 \text{ eV}$$

The frequency of this light can be calculated

since $\qquad E = hf$

then $\qquad f = \dfrac{E}{h} = \dfrac{(13.2 \text{ eV})(1.6 \times 10^{-19} \text{ J} / \text{eV})}{6.63 \times 10^{-34} \text{ J} \cdot \text{s}}$ ← convert eV to J

$$= 3.19 \times 10^{15} \text{ Hz} \quad \text{This is an ultraviolet}$$

frequency.

The wavelength is $\qquad \lambda = \dfrac{c}{f} = \dfrac{3.00 \times 10^8 \text{ m} / \text{s}}{3.19 \times 10^{15} \text{ Hz}}$

$$= 9.40 \times 10^{-8} \text{ m}$$

This wavelength corresponds to a wavelength in the Lyman series of the hydrogen spectrum.

2. It can go from n = 6 to n = 2, and then from n = 2 to n = 1 (n = 6 to n = 1 in two jumps). Each jump will produce a photon.

for n = 6 to n = 2: $\qquad E = E_6 - E_2 = 3.02 \text{ eV}$

The frequency of this photon is 7.3×10^{14} Hz (violet light).

for n = 2 to n = 1: $\qquad E = E_2 - E_1 = 10.2 \text{ eV}$

The frequency of this photon is 2.46×10^{15} Hz (UV. light).

3. It can go from n = 6 $\rightarrow$ n = 4 $\rightarrow$ n = 2 $\rightarrow$ n = 1

photon
$E = 0.47$ eV
f =infrared

photon
$E = 2.55$ eV
f =visible

photon
$E = 10.2$ eV
f =ultraviolet

4. It may go from $n = 6 \to n = 5 \to n = 4 \to n = 3 \to n = 2 \to n = 1$, emitting a photon at each jump.

photon   photon   photon   photon   photon

It can easily be demonstrated that when an electron moves from any orbit greater than $n = 2$, and stops at $n = 2$, a photon of light is emitted with a frequency corresponding to a line in the Balmer series of the hydrogen spectrum. If the electron goes from:

$n = 3 \to n = 2$ red light (red line in hydrogen series)

$n = 4 \to n = 2$ green line

$n = 5 \to n = 2$ blue line   **Balmer series**

$n = 6 \to n = 2$ violet line

$n = 7 \to n = 2$ ultraviolet line

$n = \infty \to n = 2$ ultraviolet lines

initial position of electron $n_i \to n_f$ final position of electron

in single jumps.

We see that if an electron jumps from any high energy state $n > 2$ to $n = 2$ in a single jump, a photon of light corresponding to a frequency in the Balmer series of the hydrogen spectrum is emitted from the atom. If an electron moves from any high level $n > 1$ to $n = 1$ in a single jump, a Lyman series line will be produced.

If $n_i > 3$ to $n = 3$ *Paschen* line produced
If initial $n > 4$ to $n = 4$ *Brackett* line produced
If initial $n > 5$ to $n = 5$ *Pfund* line produced

Theoretically, many more series exist, but if they do, they have never been detected. Therefore Bohr says Balmer's equation is simply an energy equation. If $E = E_i - E_f$, but if $E_i = \dfrac{E_1}{n_i^2}$ and $E_f = \dfrac{E_1}{n_f^2}$, then the energy of the emitted photon is

$$E = E_i - E_f$$

$$E = \frac{E_1}{n_i^2} - \frac{E_1}{n_f^2}$$

factor out E_1 $\qquad E = E_1\left(\dfrac{1}{n_i^2} - \dfrac{1}{n_f^2}\right)$

factor out (-1) $\qquad E = -E_1\left(\dfrac{1}{n_f^2} - \dfrac{1}{n_i^2}\right)$

and since $\qquad E = hf$

then $\qquad hf = -E_1\left(\dfrac{1}{n_f^2} - \dfrac{1}{n_i^2}\right)$

and since $\qquad f = \dfrac{c}{\lambda}$

$$h\frac{c}{\lambda} = -E_1\left(\frac{1}{n_f^2} - \frac{1}{n_i^2}\right)$$

move hc to right side of equation

$$\frac{1}{\lambda} = -\frac{E_1}{hc}\left(\frac{1}{n_f^2} - \frac{1}{n_i^2}\right)$$

and this equation is simply Balmer's equation, since

$$\frac{-E_1}{hc} = R_H = \text{Rydberg's constant}$$

---

so
$$\frac{1}{\lambda} = R_H \left(\frac{1}{n_f^{\ 2}} - \frac{1}{n_i^{\ 2}} \right)$$

Balmer's equation was discovered by accident. Bohr was able to derive the equation using quantum theory. Using this theory, it is possible to determine the λ's of all of the lines in the emission spectrum of hydrogen. In fact, the Lyman series, Brackett series, and Pfund series were detected after Bohr's theory predicted their existence. Bohr's theory does not predict λ's of lines that do not exist. It accounts for all lines in the hydrogen spectrum.

Bohr's third postulate dealt with the angular momentum of the electron. Angular momentum is the momentum of an object traveling in a circular orbit of radius R. Bohr believed that electrons had an angular momentum $= mvR =$ (mass)(instantaneous velocity)(radius) that was

quantized, or packaged into amounts $= \dfrac{nh}{2\pi}$, where n = 1, 2, 3, ...

That is, an electron could have an angular momentum $= \dfrac{1h}{2\pi}$, or $\dfrac{2h}{2\pi}$, etc.

He used this information to determine the allowable radii

$$r_n = n^2 \, (r_1)$$

and the allowable energies

$$E_n = \frac{E_1}{n^2}$$

Bohr's model of the atom is called the **stationary state model**, or **Rutherford- Bohr model** of the atom. Bohr believed an atom is much like Rutherford described, but the electrons must be located only in certain allowable orbits, or **stationary energy states**.

In a picture

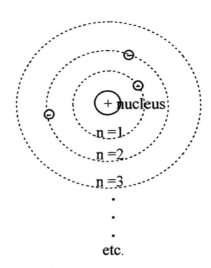

etc.

Bohr then believed that it was possible to explain electron arrangements in more complex atoms in terms of the energy states. The electrons arrange themselves in *shells* around the nucleus. There is a maximum number of electrons that may be held in each shell.

$$\text{number of electrons} = 2n^2$$

therefore $n = 1$ (first shell) $= 2(1)^2 = 2$ electrons max.

$n = 2$ (second shell)$= 2(2)^2 = 8$ electrons max.

$n = 3$ (third shell) $= 2(3)^2 = 18$ electrons max.

etc.

Electrons in any atom will occupy lowest energy levels first. Therefore, a sodium atom with 11p and 11e would have:

$$
\begin{array}{lll}
2e & in & n = 1 \\
8e & in & n = 2 \\
\underline{1e} & \underline{in} & n = 3 \\
11e & &
\end{array}
$$

The electron arrangement idea becomes quite complex, but Bohr does show how electron arrangement can determine chemical behaviour of elements.

Hydrogen atom

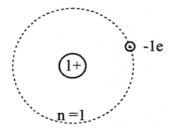

Lithium atom

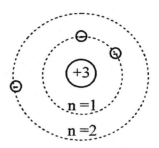

nucleus = 1 proton = +1e
1 electron outside nucleus.

nucleus = 3p = +3e
3 electrons: 2 in n = 1 (full shell)
1 in n = 2

If first shell + nucleus counted as a "core", or nucleus together, then

Lithium atom

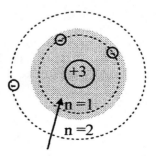

+1e nucleus
1 electron

Very similar structure to hydrogen atom.

⇒ similar chemical behaviour

PHYSICS GRADE 12

A sodium atom, with similar chemical behavior to hydrogen and lithium would have n =1 full, n = 2 full, and 1 electron outside of the +1e inner core, if the core included the 11 protons in the nucleus and the 2 full inner shells of 2e and 8e = 10e.

Bohr believed that it was the number of electrons in the outermost allowable orbit that determined chemical behaviour of elements. Today, we call these electrons **valence electrons**, and this concept together with Bohr's atom are used to explain chemistry.

So Bohr's theory was successful at

1- predicting spectra for hydrogen gas

2- explaining periodicity of elements chemical properties

3- combining the ideas of Dalton, Thompson, Rutherford, and quantum theory, that together give us a good picture of "What is an atom, and how does it work ?"

Yet, Bohr's theory did have problems!

1- it only worked at predicting the spectra with 1 valence electron

2- it did not suggest why some spectral lines in a give spectrum are relatively brighter than others.

3- no explanation given as to why atoms don't collapse. Only the assumption that they don't.

4- some ideas in Bohr's theory are untestable, so no way of knowing if these ideas are correct or not.

Bohr's theory falls short of answering all our questions about atoms, yet Bohr's theory is heralded as one of the great theories in physics today. Inconsistencies between experimental observations and theoretical predictions meant that Bohr's model of the atom could be improved.

In 1914, James Franck and Gustav Hertz showed experimentally that atoms can absorb and emit only certain energies, as predicted by Bohr's theory. They showed that when electron with given energies collided with mercury atoms, that those atoms would only absorb discrete amounts of energy.

If an electron has 1 eV, 2 eV, 3 eV, or 4 eV of energy when it collided with a mercury atom, the atom would absorb none of the energy, and the atom would "bounce off" keeping all of its energy. But if the electron had 5 eV of energy, then the atom absorbs 4.9 eV. The electron would rebound with only 0.1 eV of energy. The mercury atom would then be excited. This energy would then be emitted from the atom as a photon of light. Franck and Hertz detected this light, and found that it corresponded to a line in the spectrum of excited mercury gas. They found that other amounts of energy could be absorbed by mercury atoms: 4.9 eV, 6.7 eV, 8.8 eV, 10.4 eV, and others. This confirmed Bohr's theory that atoms will absorb and emit only certain amounts or energy.

In 1897, when J. J. Thompson discovered the electron, he noticed that as the accelerating voltage was increased for the cathode ray beam (for which he measured q/m), the value of the ratio decreased. As the speed of the electrons in the cathode beam increased, the charge-to-mass ratio decreased.

As Thompson believed and showed that q remained constant at all speeds, the mass of the electron had to be increasing as the speed of the electrons increased. This result was also predicted in 1905 by Albert Einstein. Einstein, in his special theory of relativity, suggested that for all masses, as v approached the speed of light, the mass of the object would approach infinity, that is, increase without limit. The mass of the object as measured by an observer at rest with respect to the moving mass would be called the relativistic mass of the object. The relativistic mass could be determined mathematically by $m = \dfrac{m_o}{\sqrt{1 - v^2/c^2}}$

In this equation,
m = relativistic mass (mass of moving object)
m_0 = rest mass (mass of object at rest)
v = speed of object
c = speed of light

Now, Einstein also suggested that m (which is always larger than m_o) can be expressed simply as $m = m_o + \Delta m$. Which, in words, says that the relativistic mass of an object is equal to its rest mass plus some increase in that mass called the change in mass (Δm). Einstein believed this increase in mass was a direct result of an increase in KE.

Therefore,
$$\Delta m \propto KE$$

$$\Delta m = k \, (KE)$$

by experimental results: k = **proportionality constant** = $1/c^2$

therefore
$$\Delta m = \frac{KE}{c^2}$$

so
$$m = m_o + \frac{KE}{c^2}$$

With this, Einstein then believed if the increase in mass was equivalent to the kinetic energy of the object, then the rest mass would have a "rest energy" equivalent to it.

If rest energy $= E_o$, then

$$m = \frac{E_o}{c^2} + \frac{\text{KE}}{c^2}$$

If $E_o + \text{KE} = $ total energy of the mass, then $= E$

$$m = \frac{E_o + \text{KE}}{c^2} = \frac{E}{c^2}$$

We more often see this equation as $E = mc^2$. This equation tells us that energy and mass are equivalent forms of the same thing. An object that has mass may be thought of as possessing energy. Energy can be thought of as having a mass equivalence.

Now, because light is energy, can we think of photons as having mass ? Well, photons have no rest mass. They never travel at speeds below c, and cannot exist if they stop. If photons strike a surface, their energy will be absorbed by the surface that they strike. Therefore we cannot stop a photon and measure its mass, but maybe it is possible to show that photons can behave like objects with mass. Now, any moving mass has a **momentum** $= p = mv$.

Can photons show that they have momentum ? Well, a photon has no mass, but it does have an energy. So for a photon, $p = mv$ can be

written as $\qquad p = \left(\dfrac{E}{c^2} \right) \cdot v \quad$ where $\quad m = \dfrac{E}{c^2}$

(by Einstein's mass-energy equivalence).

Now, photons only travel at c, therefore, $v = c$.

and
$$p = \frac{E}{c^2} \cdot c$$

so
$$\boxed{p = \frac{E}{c}}$$

$p \propto E$

A photon's momentum is directly related to its energy.

the energy of a photon = $E = hf$,

so
$$p = \frac{hf}{c}$$

$p \propto f$

A photon's momentum is directly related to its frequency.

the frequency of a photon = $f = \frac{c}{\lambda}$,

so
$$p = \frac{h}{c} \cdot \frac{c}{\lambda}$$

$$\boxed{p = \frac{h}{\lambda}}$$

A photon's momentum is inversely related to its wavelength.

Wave-Particle Dualism

In 1933, Arthur Compton showed that the momentum of a photon could be transferred to an object like an electron. He directed a beam of x-rays with a single frequency through a thin sheet of metal. He found that the scattered beam on the other side had two frequencies. One set of x-rays had the same frequency as before and remained unchanged, but the other set had a lower frequency, indicating a loss in momentum (and energy). He also found that some electrons had been knocked out of the metal. The momentum gained by the electrons when in collisions with x-ray photons was exactly equal to the momentum lost by the photons. This effect is called the **Compton Effect**, and shows that the photons can exhibit behavior similar to particles. That is:

> 1- they carry their energy in packages, like bullets fired from a gun.

> 2- they have momentum that can be transferred to particles.

But still, photons exhibit wave behavior as well:

> 1- they have wave characteristics like a wavelength, period, frequency, and amplitude.

> 2- they can diffract (bend around corners) and interfere, producing interference patterns.

> 3- they can be polarized.

So physicists today believe that light (EM radiation) transfers energy through space as waves, and also as particles. They refer to this as the **wave-particle dualism** for radiation. Both behaviors can be demonstrated.

- *Wave Behavior*
- diffraction
- interference
- polarization

Particle Behavior
- photoelectric effect (energy in packages: $E = hf$)
- Compton's effect (momentum: $p = \dfrac{h}{\lambda}$)

If photons can behave like waves or particles, maybe particles like electrons, protons, neutrons, etc., can demonstrate wave behaviour as well.

In 1923, **Louis de Broglie** suggested that if a photon of light has a momentum that depended upon its wavelength, then a particle (like an electron) could have a wavelength that depended upon its momentum.

Since $\qquad p = \dfrac{h}{\lambda} \qquad$ for photons,

then $\qquad \lambda = \dfrac{h}{p} \qquad$ for electrons. But $p = mv$,

therefore $\qquad \lambda = \dfrac{h}{mv}$.

This λ is called the **de Broglie wavelength**.

In 1927, it was demonstrated by G. P. Thomson that electrons will give a diffraction pattern similar to that of x-rays, with a wavelength similar to that of the electron correctly given by the above formula. So **the wave-particle dualism** holds for matter as well.

What does it mean for an electron to have a wavelength ? These "**matter waves**" are hard to imagine. It may be sufficient to say that a particle like an electron has a wavelength associated with it. The electron may exist in an allowable orbit as:

1- a wave, or

2- it may move in a wave like motion.

In either case, the wave has to "fit" the orbit. The electron moving in a wave-like motion would exist only as a standing wave, or we might say that a complete orbit must contain a whole number of wavelengths.

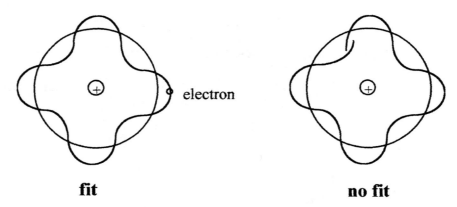

fit   **no fit**

A necessary condition for the electron to travel in such an orbit means that the circumference = C = $2\pi R$ must equal 1λ, or 2λ, or 3λ, etc., or mathematically, $2\pi R = n\lambda$,   where n = 1, 2, 3, ...

Now, since the λ must equal $\dfrac{h}{mv}$ according to de Broglie's wave equation.

then $2\pi R = n\dfrac{h}{mv}$

By rearranging this equation, we find the relation

$$mvR = \frac{nh}{2\pi}, \text{ where } n = 1, 2, 3, ...$$

This tells us that the angular momentum (*mvR*) *is* quantized into

packages of $\dfrac{1h}{2\pi}$, or $\dfrac{2h}{2\pi}$, or $\dfrac{3h}{2\pi}$, etc., just as Bohr had postulated (Recall Bohr's third postulate).

Therefore, we have two ways to think of electrons:

1- as a **particle** orbiting a nucleus with an angular momentum that is quantized, or

2- as a standing de Broglie **wave** occupying a region of space around the nucleus.

Because particles like protons, neutrons, alpha-particles and others (on an atomic scale) do demonstrate wave behaviour, the modern model of the atom, called the **quantum mechanical model**, is based upon these matter waves. The new model, unfortunately for our imagination, is a **mathematical model** that uses equations to predict atomic behaviour. This model does not give us a picture of what an atom is, but it completely describes the behaviour of atoms. This model includes Newton's theories of motion (classical theories), plus Maxwell's theory of electromagnetism, quantum theory, Einstein's special theory of relativity, and also de Broglie's matter wave theory. A comprehensive understanding of atoms using this model requires years of training in nuclear physics.

PHYSICS GRADE 12

Names and Dates That You Should Know

1800	*Alessandro Volta*	- discovered how to produce an electric current using electrochemical cell.
1808-1810	*John Dalton*	- revived ancient atomic theory to make first modern theory of atoms. - determined relative atoms masses of each element. - "Billiard Ball" model of the atom.
1810	*Thomas Young*	- determined the wavelength of light using double-slit apparatus.
1870	*Dmitri Mendeleev*	- invented the periodic table.
1875	*Sir William Crookes*	- identified properties of cathode rays.
1887	*Heinrich Hertz*	- produced first radio waves. - discovered the photoelectric effect.
1895	*Wilhelm Röntgen*	- discovered x-rays and determined their properties.
1897	*J. J. Thompson*	- identified cathode rays as electrons. - 'Raisin Bun" model of the atom.

1905	*Albert Einstein*	- used quantum theory to explain photoelectric effect. - mass-energy equivalence $(E = mc^2)$
1910-1912	*Ernest Rutherford*	- discovered nucleus of atom through scattering experiments. - "Planetary" model of the atom.
1913	*Neils Bohr*	- Bohr model of the atom - "Stationary State" model - explains spectrum of hydrogen - explains electron arrangements and chemical behaviour.
1914	*James Franck* *Gustav Hertz*	- verified Bohr's theory experimentally.
1922	*Erwin Schrodinger*	- used wave equations to define wave properties for electrons incorporated into the modern model of the atom - the "quantum mechanical", or "wave mechanics" theory.
1922	*Arthur Compton*	- showed photons have momentum.
1922	*Louis de Broglie*	- wave equation for matter waves $(\lambda = \dfrac{h}{mv})$.
1927	*G. P. Thomson*	- showed wave properties for electrons.

PHYSICS GRADE 12

The Structure of Matter Solved Problems

1. The experimental value of q/m for a proton is 9.6 x 10⁷ C/kg. What is the value of q/m for an α-particle ?

Answer: Since an α-particle is a helium nucleus, it has a charge that is 2x that of a proton and a mass that is 4x that of a proton.

Since, q/m for proton $= 9.6 \times 10^7$ C/kg

then $\dfrac{q \times 2}{m \times 4} = \left(\dfrac{q}{m}\right)\left(\dfrac{2}{4}\right) = 9.6 \times 10^7$ C/kg $\left(\dfrac{2}{4}\right)$

$= 4.8 \times 10^7$ C/kg

the q/m ratio for α-particles is 4.8 x 10⁷ C/kg.

or

for an α-particle, $q = 2\,(2.6 \times 10^{-19}\,\text{C}) = 3.2 \times 10^{-31}$ C

$m = 6.65 \times 10^{-27}$ kg

therefore, $\dfrac{q}{m} = \dfrac{3.2 \times 10^{-19}\ \text{C}}{6.65 \times 10^{-27}\ \text{kg}} =$ **4.8 x 10⁷ C/kg**

2. If the intensity of the incident light is increased in a photoelectric experiment, what is the effect on the photoelectric current, and on the energy of the photoelectrons ?

Answer: The intensity of the light controls the number of photons (of energy $= hf$) that will reach the surface per second. Then if each releases one photoelectron by increasing the intensity, the photons/second will increase, thereby increasing the number of photon electrons.

$$\frac{\# \text{ photons}}{s} = \frac{\# \text{ photoelectrons}}{s}$$

Since each electron carries a charge, than a greater charge/second will be emitted. Since I = q/t, then **the current increases**. Also, since the frequency of the light must be increased to increase the KE of the photoelectrons, if the frequency remains constant, then the **energy of the photoelectrons does not change**.

3. What is the maximum KE of emitted photoelectrons if light with a frequency of 9.2 x 10^{14} Hz strikes a surface that has a work function of 2.8 eV ?

Answer: The energy of 1 photon of this light is

$$E = hf = (6.63 \text{ x } 10^{-34} \text{ J s})(9.2 \text{ x } 10^{14} \text{ Hz})$$

$$= 6.1 \text{ x } 10^{-19} \text{ J}.$$

This energy in electron volts is

$$\frac{6.1 \text{ x } 10^{-19} \text{ J}}{1.6 \text{ x } 10^{-19} \text{ J/eV}} = 3.8 \text{ eV}$$

When this photon is absorbed by an electron, the electron will escape with a KE$_{max}$ that is the difference between the energy absorbed minus the energy lost to work.

Therefore,

$$KE_{max} = hf - W = 3.8 \text{ eV} - 2.8 \text{ eV}$$

$$= \mathbf{1.0 \text{ eV}}$$

4. An electron makes a transition from the 5ʰ energy level of a hydrogen atom to ground state. What is the wavelength of the emitted radiation ?

Answer: The electron is moving from n = 5 to n = 1. According to

Bohr, the frequency of the emitted radiation is dependent on the

energy difference between the two states, or

$$hf = E_5 - E_1 \qquad (E = E_i - E_f)$$

but $\qquad E_5 = \dfrac{E_1}{5^2} \qquad$ and $\qquad E_1 = -13.6 \text{ eV}$

so $\qquad E_5 = \dfrac{-13.6 \text{ eV}}{25} = 0.544 \text{ eV}$

Therefore,

$$hf = 0.554 \text{ eV} - (-13.6 \text{ eV}) = 13.06 \text{ eV}$$

$$f = \frac{13.06 \text{ eV}}{h} = \frac{13.06 \text{ eV}(1.6 \times 10^{-19} \text{ J/eV})}{6.63 \times 10^{-34} \text{ J s}} \quad \text{(convert eV to J)}$$

$$= 3.15 \times 10^{15} \text{ Hz} \qquad \text{(ultraviolet light)}$$

so $\qquad \lambda = \dfrac{c}{f} = \dfrac{3 \times 10^8 \text{ m/s}}{3.15 \times 10^{15} \text{ Hz}} = 0.95 \times 10^{-7} \text{ m}$

$$\mathbf{= 9.5 \times 10^{-8} \text{ m}}$$

or

use Balmer's equation

$$\frac{1}{\lambda} = R_H \left(\frac{1}{n_f{}^2} - \frac{1}{n_i{}^2} \right) \quad n_f = 1, n_i = 5$$

Lyman series.

---

5. If 5.1 eV of energy are required to remove the outermost electron in a sodium atom, and if an electron traveling at 1.5 x 10⁶ m/s strikes sodium ion and ionizes it, then what would be the maximum KE of the incident electron after the collision ?

Answer: Since the energy needed to remove the sodium electron comes from the KE of the incident electron, we must first find the KE of that electron.

$$KE = \frac{1}{2}mv^2 = \frac{1}{2}(9.11 \times 10^{-31} \text{ kg})(1.5 \times 10^6 \text{ m/s})^2$$
$$= 10.2 \times 10^{-19} \text{ J} = 1.02 \times 10^{-18} \text{ J}$$

This energy in eV is $\dfrac{1.02 \times 10^{-18} \text{ J}}{1.6 \times 10^{-19} \text{ J/eV}} = 6.4 \text{ eV}$

Since 5.1 eV are to be taken by the sodium electron, then only

6.4 eV - 5.1 eV = **1.3 eV of KE** could remain

6. A nickel surface has a work function of 5.0 eV. If this surface is illuminated with UV light with a wavelength of 2.0 x 10⁻⁷ m, then what is the stopping voltage required to stop the most energetic photons ?

Answer: It is possible to know the KE_{max} of the photoelectron from

$$KE_{max} = hf - W, \quad \text{but} \quad f = \frac{c}{\lambda}$$

therefore $\quad KE_{max} = \dfrac{hc}{\lambda} - W \quad$ and

$$\frac{hc}{\lambda} = \frac{(6.63 \times 10^{-34} \text{ J s})(3.9 \times 10^8 \text{ m/s})}{2.0 \times 10^{-7} \text{ m}} = \frac{9.945 \times 10^{-19} \text{ J}}{1.6 \times 10^{-19} \text{ J/eV}} = 6.2 \text{ eV}$$

so $\quad KE_{max} = 6.2 \text{ eV} - 5.0 \text{ eV} = 1.3 \text{ eV}$

Now since $\quad KE_{max} = qV_{stop}$

then $\quad V_{stop} = \dfrac{KE_{max}}{q} = \dfrac{1.2 \text{ eV}}{1 \text{ e}} = \textbf{1.2 V}$

7. *A charged object remains suspended in an electric field. If the object has a mass of 3.0 x 10^-14 kg, and the electric field intensity is 6.1 x 10^4 N/C, then*
a) *What is the net charge on the object ?*

Answer: To be suspended

$$F_e = F_g$$
$$q|E| = mg$$
$$q = \frac{mg}{|E|}$$
$$= \frac{(3.0 \times 10^{-14}\,\text{kg})(9.81\,\text{N/kg})}{6.1 \times 10^{-18}\,\text{N/C}}$$
$$= \mathbf{4.82 \times 10^{-18}\,C}$$

b) *If the object is negatively charged, how many excess electrons are on it ?*

Answer: number of electrons $= \dfrac{\text{total net charge}}{\text{charge per electron}} = \dfrac{4.82 \times 10^{-18}\,\text{C}}{1.6 \times 10^{-19}\,\text{C/e}}$

$$= \mathbf{30e}$$

8. *In an x-ray tube, electrons are accelerated across a potential difference, V, when upon striking the anode, the KE of the electron is emitted as a photon or KE = E = hf_max . What is the relationship between the minimum wavelength of the emitted x-ray and the accelerating voltage ?*

Answer: Since $\quad f_{max} = \dfrac{c}{\lambda_{min}} \quad$ then $\quad E = \dfrac{hc}{\lambda_{min}}$

The KE gained by the accelerating electron is

$$KE_{gain} = qV$$

therefore
$$KE = E$$
$$qV = \frac{hc}{\lambda_{min}}$$

$$qV = \frac{hc}{\lambda_{min}}$$

$$\lambda_{min} = \frac{hc}{qV}$$

therefore

$$\lambda_{min} \propto \frac{1}{V}$$

There is an **inverse relationship** between λ_{min} and V.

9. *An electron passes through perpendicular electric and magnetic field of strengths 3.80 x 10^6 N/C and 4.90 x 10^{-2} T respectively. What is the radius of the arc through which the electron would travel if it passed through only the magnetic field ?*

Answer: As seen with J. J. Thompson's cathode ray tube that he used

to   determine the q/m ratio for electrons, the strengths of the two

fields   can be used to determine the speed, v, of the electron.

Because $F_e = F_m$

$$\cancel{q}|E| = \cancel{q}vB$$

$$v = \frac{|E|}{B} = \frac{3.80 \times 10^6\,\text{N/C}}{4.90 \times 10^{-2}\,\text{T}} = 7.76 \times 10^7\,\text{m/s}$$

Now, if B is operating alone, then the magnetic force is acting

perpendicular to v, and is then a centripetal force.

So $F_m = F_c$

$$q\cancel{v}B = \frac{mv^2}{R}$$

$$R = \frac{mv}{qB} = \frac{(9.11 \times 10^{-31}\,\text{kg})(7.76 \times 10^7\,\text{m/s})}{(1.6 \times 10^{-19}\,\text{C})(4.90 \times 10^{-2}\,\text{T})}$$

$$= \mathbf{9.01 \times 10^{-3}\,m}$$

10. A photon with a 16.4 eV of energy strikes an electron in a hydrogen atom and ionizes it. What is the kinetic energy of the ejected electron ?

Answer: It requires 13.6 eV to ionize an electron from ground state in a hydrogen atom. Therefore, since all the energy must be absorbed by the electron, the first 13.6 eV of energy would take the electron from n =1 to n = ∞, the remaining energy would be KE of ejected electron, or

$$16.4 \text{ eV} - 13.6 \text{ eV} = \textbf{2.8 eV}.$$

11. A photon of wavelength 7.8×10^{-10} m strikes an electron at rest, and gives is 2.9×10^{-17} J of energy. What is the λ of the departing photon ?

Answer: The energy of the photon is

$$E = hf = \frac{hc}{\lambda} = \frac{(6.63 \times 10^{-34} \text{ J} \cdot \text{s})(3.00 \times 10^{8} \text{ m/s})}{7.8 \times 10^{-10} \text{ m}}$$
$$= 2.55 \times 10^{-16} \text{ J}$$

Some of this energy is lost. Therefore,

energy of departing photon = 2.55×10^{-16} J - 2.9×10^{-17} J

cannot subtract unless powers are equal

$$= 2.55 \times 10^{-16} \text{ J} - 0.29 \times 10^{-16} \text{ J}$$
$$= 2.26 \times 10^{-16} \text{ J}$$

Since this is the energy of the departing photon,

and $\qquad\qquad E = \dfrac{hc}{\lambda}$

$$\lambda = \frac{hc}{E} = \frac{(6.63 \times 10^{-34} \text{ J} \cdot \text{s})(3.00 \times 10^{8} \text{ m/s})}{2.26 \times 10^{-16} \text{ J}}$$
$$= \textbf{8.8} \times \textbf{10}^{-10} \textbf{ m}$$

12. *A photon has a period of 8.50 x 10^{-15} s. What is its momentum ?*

Answer:
$$p = \frac{h}{\lambda} = \frac{hf}{c} \quad \text{but} \quad f = \frac{1}{T} \quad \text{so} \quad p = \frac{hf}{c} = \frac{h}{c}(f) = \frac{h}{c}\left(\frac{1}{T}\right)$$

and
$$p = \frac{h}{cT} = \frac{6.63 \times 10^{-34} \text{ J} \cdot \text{s}}{(3.00 \times 10^{8} \text{ m/s})(8.50 \times 10^{-15}\text{s})}$$

$$= 0.26 \times 10^{-28} \text{ kg m/s}$$

$$= \mathbf{2.60 \times 10^{-29} \text{ kg m/s}}$$

PHYSICS GRADE 12

The Structure of Matter Practice Problems

1. An electric field of 5.6×10^5 N/C is perpendicular to a magnetic field of intensity 1.4×10^{-2} T. If an electron can pass undeflected through both fields simultaneously, then what is the speed of the electron ?

2. Determine the radius of the 5th Bohr orbit of a hydrogen atom.

3. An electron is to be used to ionize a hydrogen atom. What would be the minimum speed needed for the electron ?

4. An alpha-particle passes horizontally, undeflected, through a vertical electric field. What is the strength of the electric field ?

5. What is the wavelength of the radiation emitted when the electron makes a transition from the 4th energy level to the second in a hydrogen atom ?

6. A photoelectric surface has a threshold frequency of 5.0×10^{14} Hz. What is the maximum KE of photoelectrons emitted if light with a $\lambda = 1.7 \times 10^{-7}$ m is incident on the surface ?

7. An electron in an x-ray tube is accelerated across a potential difference of 4.2×10^3 V. What is the frequency of the x-ray produced ?

8. What happens to the q/m ratio for an electron as the speed of the electron increases ?

9. What is the speed of an electron that has the same momentum as a photon with $\lambda = 6.8 \times 10^{-7}$ m ?

10. What is the λ of an electron that accelerates from rest through a potential difference of 250 V ?

PHYSICS GRADE 12

The Structure of Matter Practice Problem Solutions

1. *An electric field of 5.6 x 10^5 N/C is perpendicular to a magnetic field of intensity 1.4 x 10^{-2} T. If an electron can pass undeflected through both fields simultaneously, then what is the speed of the electron?*

Answer:
$$F_e = F_m$$
$$q|E| = qvB$$
$$v = \frac{|E|}{B} = \frac{5.6 \times 10^5 \, \text{N/C}}{1.4 \times 10^{-2} \, \text{T}} = \textbf{4 x } 10^7 \textbf{ m/s}$$

2. *Determine the radius of the 5th Bohr orbit of a hydrogen atom.*

Answer:
$$v_5 = n^2 \, (r_1)$$
$$= 5^2 \, (5.3 \times 10^{-11} \, \text{m})$$
$$= 25(5.3 \times 10^{-11} \, \text{m})$$
$$= 132.5 \times 10^{-11} \, \text{m}$$
$$= \textbf{1.3 x } 10^{-9} \textbf{ m}$$

3. An electron is to be used to ionize a hydrogen atom. What would be the minimum speed needed for the electron ?

Answer: To ionize a hydrogen atom, the incoming electron would need to give the atom 13.6 eV of energy to remove the electron from the hydrogen atom.

Therefore,

$$KE = 13.6 \text{ eV}$$
$$= 13.6 \text{ eV}(1.6 \times 10^{-19} \text{ J/eV})$$
$$= 21.76 \times 10^{-19} \text{ J}$$

Since

$$KE = \frac{1}{2}mv^2$$

$$v^2 = \frac{2KE}{m}$$

$$v = \sqrt{\frac{2KE}{m}} = \sqrt{\frac{2(21.76 \times 10^{-19} \text{ J})}{9.11 \times 10^{-31} \text{ kg}}}$$

$$= \sqrt{4.78 \times 10^{12} \text{ m}^2/\text{s}^2} = \textbf{2.18 x 10}^6 \textbf{ m/s}$$

4. An alpha-particle passes horizontally, undeflected, through a vertical electric field. What is the strength of the electric field ?

Answer:

$$F_e = F_g$$
$$q|E| = mg$$
$$|E| = \frac{mg}{q}$$
$$= \frac{(6.65 \times 10^{-27} \text{ kg})(9.81 \text{ m/s}^2)}{(3.2 \times 10^{-19} \text{ C})}$$
$$= 20.4 \times 10^{-8} \text{ N/C} = \textbf{2.04 x 10}^{-7} \textbf{ N/C}$$

5. *What is the wavelength of the radiation emitted when the electron makes a transition from the 4th energy level to the second in a hydrogen atom ?*

Answer:

$$\frac{1}{\lambda} = R_H \left(\frac{1}{n_f^2} - \frac{1}{n_i^2} \right)$$

$$\frac{1}{\lambda} = (1.1 \times 10^7 / \text{m}) \left(\frac{1}{2^2} - \frac{1}{4^2} \right) = (1.1 \times 10^7 / \text{m}) \left(\frac{1}{4} - \frac{1}{16} \right)$$

$$= (1.1 \times 10^7 / \text{m}) \left(\frac{4}{16} - \frac{1}{16} \right) = (1.1 \times 10^7 / \text{m}) \left(\frac{3}{16} \right)$$

therefore,

$$\lambda = \frac{16}{(1.1 \times 10^7 / \text{m})(3)} = \textbf{4.85 x 10}^{-7} \textbf{ m}$$

6. *A photoelectric surface has a threshold frequency of 5.0 x 10^{14} Hz. What is the maximum KE of photoelectrons emitted if light with a λ =1.7 x 10^{-7} m is incident on the surface ?*

Answer: f of incident light $= \dfrac{c}{\lambda} = \dfrac{3 \times 10^8 \text{ m/s}}{1.7 \times 10^{-7} \text{m}} = $ 1.76 x 10^{15} Hz

$\text{KE}_{max} = hf - hf_o = h\,(f - f_o) = h\,(1.76 \text{ x } 10^{15} \text{ Hz} - 0.5 \text{ x } 10^{15} \text{ Hz})$

$= h\,(1.26 \text{ x } 10^{15} \text{ Hz})$

$= (6.63 \text{ x } 10^{-34} \text{ J s})(1.26 \text{ x } 10^{15} \text{ Hz})$

$= \textbf{8.4 x 10}^{-19} \textbf{ J}$

7. *An electron in an x-ray tube is accelerated across a potential difference of 4.2 x 10³ V. What is the frequency of the x-ray produced ?*

Answer:
$$hf_{max} = qV$$

$$f_{m,ax} = \frac{qV}{h} = \frac{(1.6 \times 10^{-19}\,C)(4.2 \times 10^{3}\,J/C)}{(6.63 \times 10^{-34}\,J\,s)} = \mathbf{1.0 \times 10^{18}}$$

Hz

8. *What happens to the q/m ratio for an electron as the speed of the electron increases ?*

Answer: Since
$$F_m = F_c$$

$$qvB = \frac{mv^2}{R}$$

$$\frac{q}{m} = \frac{v}{BR}$$
since $\frac{q}{m} \propto v$, **as *v* increases,**

q/*m* should increase directly.

9. *What is the speed of an electron that has the same momentum as a photon with λ = 6.8 x 10⁻⁷ m ?*

Answer:
$$p_{photon} = \frac{h}{\lambda} = \frac{6.63 \times 10^{-34}\,J\,s}{6.8 \times 10^{-7}\,m} = 0.975 \times 10^{-27}\,kg\,m/s$$

$$= 9.75 \times 10^{-28}\,kg\,m/s$$

If electron has $p = 9.75 \times 10^{-28}$ kg m/s, and $p = mv$, then

$$v = \frac{p}{m} = \frac{9.75 \times 10^{-28}\,kg\,m/s}{9.11 \times 10^{-31}\,kg} = \mathbf{1.07 \times 10^{3}\,m/s}$$

10. *What is the λ of an electron that accelerates from rest through a potential difference of 250 V ?*

Answer: $\lambda = \dfrac{h}{p} = \dfrac{h}{mv}$ we need to know v.

Since electron gain

$$KE = qV$$

$$\frac{1}{2}mv^2 = qV$$

$$v^2 = \frac{2qV}{m}$$

so $v = \sqrt{\dfrac{2qV}{m}} = \sqrt{\dfrac{2(1.6 \times 10^{-19}\,\text{C})(250\,\text{V})}{9.11 \times 10^{-31}\,\text{kg}}}$

$$= \sqrt{87.8 \times 10^{12}\,\text{m}^2/\text{s}^2}$$

$$= 9.37 \times 10^6 \text{ m/s}$$

Therefore

$$\lambda = \frac{h}{mv} = \frac{6.63 \times 10^{-34}\,\text{J s}}{(9.11 \times 10^{-31}\,\text{kg})(9.37 \times 10^6\,\text{m/s})}$$

$$= 0.07777 \times 10^{-9} \text{ m}$$

$$= \mathbf{7.78 \times 10^{-11} \text{ m}}$$

PHYSICS GRADE 12

RADIOACTIVITY

Radioactive Decay

In 1896, Henri Becquerel discovered radioactivity. He found that uranium could expose photographic paper even when the paper was enclosed in opaque paper, or even wrapped with sheets of metal. Uranium emits high frequency electromagnetic radiation spontaneously. Any element that does this is called a **radioactive element.** Polonium and radium are other examples of radioactive elements.

Many elements have radioactive **isotopes.** An isotope is an atom of any element that varies in the number of neutrons found in the nucleus. For example: carbon atoms always have 6 protons in their nuclei, but the number of neutrons may commonly be 6, 7 or 8. Therefore the different isotopes have different atomic masses. For carbon, the most common isotopes are $^{12}_{6}C$, $^{13}_{6}C$ and $^{14}_{6}C$. $^{12}_{6}C$ is typical for most carbon atoms. $^{13}_{6}C$ is rare. $^{14}_{6}C$ is rare and radioactive.

The nucleus of a radioactive atom, for reasons unknown to man, will spontaneously **decay** (possibly to achieve a more stable nucleus), **or break apart**, producing an altered nucleus. The altered nucleus may also decay. A series of decays is possible. When a nucleus decays it emits different forms of radiation. Ernest Rutherford determined that there were three types:

1 - high speed, positively charged particles that he named

α–particles (alpha-particles).

2 - high speed, negatively charged particles that he named β–particles (beta-particles).

3 - high frequency, EM radiation that he named γ-radiation/rays (gamma-rays).

Since then it has been determined that:

1 - α–particles are **helium nuclei** ($^4_2$He - mass 4 amu and charge of +2e)

2 - β–particles are **electrons** ($^0_{-1}$e)

3 - γ-rays are **EM waves**, more energetic, and of higher frequency than x-rays.

Each of the three types of radiation have different abilities to penetrate matter.

1 - α–particles can be stopped by a thin sheet of aluminum. They are also stopped after passing through a few centimeters of air.

2 - β–particles (with very high speeds) require several centimeters of aluminum to stop them. It requires a few meters of air to stop these particles.

3 - γ-rays can pass through 30 cm of steel and nearly a meter of aluminum. They travel at **c** and travel through space and air easily. γ-rays are an extremely dangerous form of radiation

as they can kill healthy cells in the body. They can also be controlled and used to irradiate and kill cancerous cells.

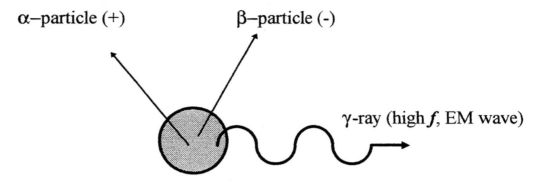

α–particle (+)   β–particle (-)

γ-ray (high f, EM wave)

Radioactive Nucleus

Why does a nucleus decay ?

The nucleus, in an effort to gain a more stable structure, will spontaneously emit particles and radiation. Therefore, an *unstable nucleus* seems to be the reason for decay to another nuclear form.

What factors contribute to instability ?

1 - *mass*: It seems that very light and very heavy elements have radioactive isotopes, and that mid-range elements have few. In the production of a nucleus, protons and neutrons come together. The mass of the nucleus is slightly less than the mass of the components from which it was formed. The missing mass is believed to be in the form of the energy that *binds* the nucleus together. This energy is therefore called the **binding energy.**

PHYSICS GRADE 12

For example: 1 helium nucleus has a mass of 4.0015 atomic mass units. It is made up of 2 neutrons (mass of 1.0087 amu each) and 2 protons (mass of 1.0073 amu each).

$2(1.0087$ amu$) + 2(1.0073$ amu$) = 4.0320$ amu

Mass balance:

2 neutrons + 2 Protons   mass = 4.0320 amu

helium nucleus   mass = <u>4.0015</u> amu

mass difference = 0.0305 amu

This mass difference is called the **mass defect** for that nucleus. Using Einstein's mass-energy equivalence relation $\mathbf{E = mc^2}$, it is possible to know the energy that binds the protons and neutrons together in the helium nucleus. It follows that if a nucleus has a large binding energy it should be stable. It turns out that very light and very heavy nuclei have the smallest binding energies, and it follows that they are less stable. Any nucleus heavier than bismuth (element # 83) is unstable.

2 - *p/n ratio:* p/n ratio is proton to neutron ratio. In the low weight nuclei, if the p/n ratio is 1, then the nucleus is stable. (Bismuth is 83/126)
In heavier nuclei the ratio of p/n for stability is lower. (0.659)

3 - *even-odd rule:* It seems that the most stable nuclei have an even number of neutrons and protons. Very few stable nuclei have both *odd* numbers of protons and neutrons.

These three factors (mass, p/n ratio, and odd-even rule) can be used to predict stability, but there are exceptions as there are general trends.

When nuclei are changed, they take part in a **nuclear reaction.**
There are four types of nuclear reactions.

1 - radioactive decomposition

2 - nuclear disintegration

3 - fission

4 - fusion   They *all* release energy.

Nuclear Equations

To study nuclear reactions, you must know how to balance a
nuclear equation.   To do this, you must remember:

1 - only nuclei are involved.

2 - the nuclei are shown with subscripts, and the sums of the
subscripts and the superscripts of the reactants must equal those of the
products.

3 - there are some symbols used for various important particles of a
nuclear reaction that should be noted:

α - alpha particle: - $^4_2\textbf{He}$

β - beta particle: - $^0_{-1}\textbf{e}$

p - proton: - $^1_1\textbf{H}$ or $^1_1\textbf{p}$

n - neutron: - $^1_0\textbf{n}$

For any nucleus, lithium for example, the symbol for the nucleus is
shown like this: $^7_3\textbf{Li.}$ Superscript = total # of protons and neutrons and Subscript = # of protons

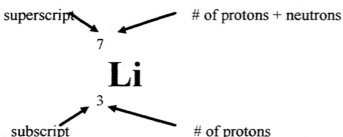

superscript → 7 ← # of protons + neutrons

Li

subscript → 3 ← # of protons

The subscript shows the number of protons found in the nucleus, and is found on the periodic table as the **atomic number.** (Showing the place for the element on the periodic table).

This tells us that the lithium nucleus has 3 protons.

The superscript shows the number of protons and neutrons in the nucleus. It can be found on some periodic tables as the **mass number.** (of the isotope of the element being considered)

This tells us that the nucleus of lithium has 7 protons and neutrons. We can now know the number of neutrons in this lithium nucleus (7-3) = 4.

Since the subscripts represent **electric charge** and the superscripts represent **mass**, then a balanced equation shows that the *electric charge* and the *mass* are conserved. The laws of conservation apply in nuclear reactions.

Radioactive Decomposition

Radioactive decomposition occurs when certain heavy nuclei spontaneously break apart (decay) into lighter nuclei. When they do this they will release alpha particle(s) and/or beta particles, and at the same time, gamma rays. This is called nuclear **transmutation.**

$^{238}_{92}U$ is an example of a nucleus that undergoes transmutation. This transmutation involves a series of alpha and beta decays until the parent nucleus has transmuted to the stable $^{206}_{82}$**Pb.**

The transmutation follows the decay path as follows:

$$^{238}_{92}U \longrightarrow \alpha + ^{234}_{90}Th \longrightarrow \beta + ^{234}_{91}Pa \longrightarrow \beta + ^{234}_{92}U \longrightarrow \alpha + ^{230}_{90}Th \longrightarrow$$

$$\longrightarrow \alpha + ^{226}_{88}Ra \longrightarrow \alpha + ^{222}_{86}Rn \longrightarrow \alpha + ^{218}_{84}Po \longrightarrow \alpha + ^{214}_{82}Pb \longrightarrow \beta + ^{214}_{83}Bi \longrightarrow$$

$$\longrightarrow \beta + ^{214}_{84}Po \longrightarrow \alpha + ^{210}_{82}Pb \longrightarrow \beta + ^{210}_{83}Bi \longrightarrow \beta + ^{210}_{84}Po \longrightarrow \alpha + ^{206}_{82}Pb$$

The entire series is a naturally occurring, radioactive decomposition series that converts $^{238}_{93}U$ nuclei into $^{206}_{82}Pb$ nuclei. All of this is achieved by the release of alpha and beta particles. This same series can be shown by a series of equations like:

$$^{238}_{92}U \longrightarrow ^{234}_{90}Th + ^{4}_{2}He + \gamma\text{-ray (energy)}$$

(remember that $^{4}_{2}He$ is an alpha-particle)

After the uranium nucleus transmutes into a thorium nucleus by emitting an alpha-particle and energy, the thorium then transmutes by beta decay into a protactinium nucleus, by the following reaction:

$$^{234}_{90}Th \longrightarrow ^{234}_{91}Pa + ^{0}_{-1}e + \text{energy}$$

(remember that $^{0}_{-1}e$ is a beta-particle, or an electron)

Other equations would be:

$$^{234}_{91}Pa \longrightarrow ^{234}_{92}U + ^{0}_{-1}e + \text{energy}$$

$$^{234}_{92}U \longrightarrow ^{230}_{90}Th + ^{4}_{2}He + \text{energy}$$

$$^{230}_{90}Th \longrightarrow ^{226}_{88}Ra + ^{4}_{2}He + \text{energy}$$

...*and so on*... (the "+energy" is often omitted, as it can be taken for granted that gamma rays will be emitted).

Notice that for each equation, - subscripts on left = subscripts on right,

and   - superscripts on left = superscripts on right.

PHYSICS GRADE 12

There are three common such decay series found in nature. The $^{238}_{92}U$ decay series is one of them.

When a sample of $^{238}_{92}U$ decays, not all of the nuclei will decay at the same moment, but over a period of time the nuclei will be altered. The time required for 1/2 of all of the nuclei in a sample to undergo decay is called the **half-life** of that isotope. Different isotopes have different half-lives.

For example: $^{238}_{92}U$ has a half-life of 2.46×10^9 years.

$^{234}_{90}$**Th** has a half-life of 24 days.

$^{14}_{6}C$ has a half-life of 5570 years.

Some isotopes have very short half lives, some in seconds and much less. Since the half-life is the time for 1/2 of the nuclei to be changed to other nuclei, it is also the time for 1/2 of the mass of the original given sample to decompose. Subsequently, after a half life has passed, only half of the original mass of the given isotope remains. After another half-life, only half of *that* mass remains, and so on..

For example: for a 60g sample of $^{14}_{6}C$ we get the following:

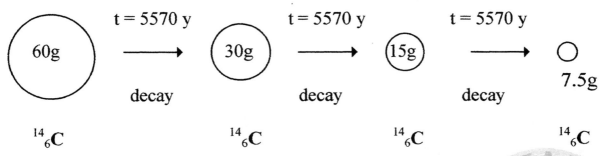

The missing mass has been transmuted into a different isotope. The decaying isotope is called the **parent** isotope. The new isotope(s) formed is called the **daughter.** Therefore the mass of the radioactive parent isotope is reduced over a period of time.

The mass remaining of the parent isotope after radioactive decay began for a given sample is given by the equation:

$$m = m_o \times \left\{ \frac{1}{2} \right\}^{t/h}$$

where: m = mass of radioactive isotope remaining after radioactive decomposition (decay) began.

m_o = original mass of radioactive isotope.

t = time that has elapsed since decay began.

h = half-life of the decaying isotope.

The mass equation may be written as:

$$m = m_o \times \left\{ \frac{1}{2} \right\}^{n}$$

where: n = the number of half-lives that have passed since decomposition began.

Since the mass depends on the number of nuclei present, it follows that:

$$N = N_o \times \left\{ \frac{1}{2} \right\}^{n}$$

where: N_o = the original number of nuclei.

N = the number of nuclei remaining.

and   n = the number of half-lives that have passed since decomposition began.

Sometimes the **activity** (A) of a radioactive sample is measured. Activity is measured in decays/ second, or **Becquerels** (Bq). Since each nucleus can decay only once, it follows that:

$$A = A_o \times \left\{ \frac{1}{2} \right\}^{n}$$

where: Ao = the original activity.

and   A = the activity after n half-lives have elapsed.

PHYSICS GRADE 12

Nuclear Disintegration

Nuclear disintegration requires the firing of a high speed projectile into the nucleus of some atom to produce a new nucleus. For example: an alpha-particle fired into a nitrogen nucleus will produce an oxygen nucleus and a proton.

$$^{14}_{7}N + \,^{4}_{2}He \longrightarrow \,^{16}_{8}O + \,^{1}_{1}H + \text{energy}$$

Some other examples are:

$$^{7}_{3}Li + \,^{1}_{1}H \longrightarrow \,^{4}_{2}He + \,^{4}_{2}He + \text{energy}$$

$$^{9}_{4}Be + \,^{4}_{2}He \longrightarrow \,^{12}_{6}C + \,^{1}_{0}n + \text{energy}$$

$$^{252}_{98}Cf + \,^{11}_{5}B \longrightarrow \,^{257}_{103}Lw + 6\,^{1}_{0}n + \text{energy}$$

(6 neutrons emitted.)

Note that the mass (superscripts) and the charge (subscripts) are conserved.

Fission

Fission reactions involve splitting a heavy nucleus into two lighter ones, releasing energy in the process.

$$^{235}_{92}U + \,^{1}_{0}n \longrightarrow \,^{141}_{56}Ba + \,^{92}_{36}Kr + 3\,^{1}_{0}n + \text{energy}$$

In this reaction, about 10% of the mass of the $^{235}_{92}U$ nucleus is emitted as energy. ($E = mc^2$). This is a large amount of energy. When the high speed neutron ($^{1}_{0}n$) strikes the uranium nucleus, it separates into two smaller parts, and at the same time, releases the neutrons that can continue to split other nuclei to set up a **chain reaction**. The **atomic bomb** that ended World War II used this reaction to generate its energy.

In today's modern nuclear reactors, fissionable $^{238}_{92}U$ (natural uranium) is used as the fuel. Its fission reaction is in two parts. (99.3% is $^{238}_{92}U$, and 0.7% is $^{235}_{92}U$)

$$^{235}_{92}U + ^{1}_{0}n \longrightarrow ^{141}_{56}Ba + ^{92}_{36}Kr + 3\,^{1}_{0}n + energy$$

and

$$^{238}_{92}U + ^{1}_{0}n \longrightarrow ^{239}_{92}U + energy$$

$$^{239}_{92}U \longrightarrow ^{239}_{93}Np + ^{0}_{-1}e + energy$$

$$^{239}_{93}Np \longrightarrow ^{239}_{94}Pu + ^{0}_{-1}e + energy$$

The reactants of such reactions produce radioactive products that are a major cause for concern today. It is difficult to dispose of Nuclear Waste.

Fusion

Energy is released when two nuclei combine to form a heavier nucleus. The Sun produces energy through such reactions, as do hydrogen bombs.

$$4\,^{1}_{1}H + 2\,^{0}_{-1}e \longrightarrow ^{4}_{2}He + energy$$

$$^{3}_{1}H + ^{2}_{1}H \longrightarrow ^{4}_{2}He + ^{1}_{0}n + energy$$

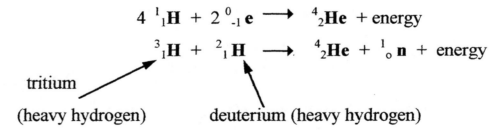

tritium
(heavy hydrogen)   deuterium (heavy hydrogen)

Fusion is a difficult reaction to achieve on Earth, because it requires very high temperatures, and extreme pressures to force the nuclei together. But once this is accomplished, tremendous amounts of energy are released. It is hoped that this reaction will one day be supplying the day-to-day energy needs of mankind, hopefully without nuclear waste.

PHYSICS GRADE 12

Radioactivity - Solved Problems

1. Strontium-90 has a half-life of 25 years. If an original sample has 60g, then after 3 half-lives have passed, what mass of strontium-90 remains?

Answer: Since $\quad\quad m = m_o \times \{ 1/2 \}^n \quad\quad n = 3$ y, $m_o = 60$g

therefore mass remaining $= m = m_o \times \{ 1/2 \}^n$

$$= 60\text{g} \times \{ 1/2 \}^3$$
$$= 60\text{g} \times 1/8$$
$$= 60/8 \text{ g}$$
$$= \mathbf{7.5 \text{ g}}$$

2. Find the missing nucleus.

a) $^6_3\text{Li} + {}^2_1\text{H} \longrightarrow {}^4_2\text{He} + ? + \text{energy}$

b) $^{35}_{17}\text{Cl} + ? \longrightarrow {}^{32}_{16}\text{S} + {}^4_2\text{He} + \text{energy}$

Answer: Since the superscripts and the subscripts must be equal

    a) $^6_3\text{Li} + {}^2_1\text{H} \longrightarrow {}^4_2\text{He} + {}^4_2\text{X} + \text{energy}$

    and ^4_2X from the periodic table is ^4_2He

    Therefore, a helium nucleus is missing from the equation.

    b) $^{35}_{17}\text{Cl} + {}^1_1\text{X} \longrightarrow {}^{32}_{16}\text{S} + {}^4_2\text{He} + \text{energy}$

    and $^1_1\text{X} = {}^1_1\text{p}$, or ^1_1H

    Therefore, a hydrogen nucleus is missing from the equation.

PHYSICS GRADE 12

Radioactivity - Practice Problems

1. The half-life for $^{24}_{11}\text{Na}$ is 1.5 hours. How many grams of sodium would remain after 75 hours if 30g was in the initial sample?

2. If 3_1H has a half-life of 12.5 years, then how many years have passed when only $1/64^{\text{th}}$ of the original mass remains?

PHYSICS GRADE 12

3. Find the missing nuclei from the following equations.

    a) $^{9}_{4}\text{Be} + \,^{4}_{2}\text{He} \longrightarrow \,^{1}_{0}\text{n} + \,? + \text{energy}$

    b) $^{14}_{7}\text{Be} + \,^{4}_{2}\text{He} \longrightarrow \,^{1}_{1}\text{H} + \,? + \text{energy}$

    c) $^{11}_{5}\text{B} + \,^{1}_{1}\text{H} \longrightarrow \,^{11}_{6}\text{C} + \,? + \text{energy}$

    d) $^{6}_{3}\text{Li} + \,? \longrightarrow \,^{7}_{4}\text{Be} + \,^{1}_{0}\text{n} + \text{energy}$

4. Find the binding energy of $^{20}_{10}\text{Ne}$ if the mass of one neon atom is 19.9924 amu, and the mass of 1 proton is 1.0073 amu, and the mass of 1 neutron is 1.0087 amu. Note: Find the mass defect, then use $E = mc^2$ to find the energy equivalence of this mass.

5. $^{235}_{92}U + ^{1}_{0}n \longrightarrow ^{140}_{54}Xe + ^{94}_{38}Sr + ? \ ^{1}_{0}n + energy$

How many neutrons are liberated in this fission reaction?

PHYSICS GRADE 12

Radioactivity - Practice Problem Solutions

1. The half-life for $^{24}_{11}Na$ is 15 hours. How many grams of sodium would remain after 75 hours if 30g was in the original sample?

Answer: $m_o = 30g$, $h = 15$ hours, $t = 75$ hours, $m_{75} = ?$

$$m_{75} = m_o \times \{1/2\}^{t/h}$$

$$= m_o \times \{2\}^{-t/h}$$

$$= 30g \times (2)^{-75/15}$$

$$= 30g \times 2^{-5} = 30g (1/32) = 30/32 \ g$$

$$= \mathbf{0.94 \ g} \text{ remaining}$$

2. If $^{3}_{1}H$ has a half-life of 12.5 years, then how many years have passed when only $1/64^{th}$ of the original mass remains?

Answer: Let m_o = the original mass. Then after t years:

$$m_t = m_o \times (2)^{-t/h}$$

$$m_t = 1/64 \ m_o = m_o \times (2)^{-t/12.5}$$

$$1/64 = 1/ \ 2^{t/12.5}$$

since $64 = 2^6$, $2^6 = 2^{t/12.5}$

and $6 = t/ \ 12.5$

therefore $t = 6(\ 12.5 \text{ years})$

$$= \mathbf{75 \ years} \text{ have passed.}$$

PHYSICS GRADE 12

3. *Find the missing nuclei from the following equations.*

Answers :
a) $^9_4\text{Be} + {}^4_2\text{He} \longrightarrow {}^1_0\text{n} + {}^{12}_6\text{C} + \text{energy}$

b) $^{14}_7\text{Be} + {}^4_2\text{He} \longrightarrow {}^1_1\text{H} + {}^{17}_8\text{O} + \text{energy}$

c) $^{11}_5\text{B} + {}^1_1\text{H} \longrightarrow {}^{11}_6\text{C} + {}^1_0\text{n} + \text{energy}$

d) $^6_3\text{Li} + {}^2_1\text{H} \longrightarrow {}^7_4\text{Be} + {}^1_0\text{n} + \text{energy}$

4. *Find the binding energy of $^{20}_{10}\text{Ne}$ if the mass of one neon atom is 19.9924 amu, and the mass of 1 proton is 1.0073 amu, and the mass of 1 neutron is 1.0087 amu. Note: Find the mass defect, then use $E = mc^2$ to find the energy equivalence of this mass.*

Answer: $^{20}_{10}\text{Ne}$ contains 10 p and 10 n.

mass of 10 p $= 10\,(1.0073\text{ amu})$
$= 10.073\text{ amu}$

mass of 10 n $= 10\,(1.0087\text{ amu})$
$= 10.087\text{ amu}$

mass of 10p + 10n $= 10.073\text{ amu} + 10.087\text{ amu}$
$= 20.160\text{ amu}$

mass of Ne atom $= \underline{19.9924\text{ amu}}$

mass defect $= 0.1676\text{ amu}$ (1 amu = 1.66×10^{-27} kg)

therefore: mass defect $= (0.1676\text{ amu}) \times (1.66 \times 10^{-27}\text{ kg/amu})$
$= 0.27 \times 10^{-27}\text{ kg}$
$= 2.7 \times 10^{-28}\text{ kg}$

Since $E = mc^2$, $E = (2.7 \times 10^{-28}\text{ kg})(3.0 \times 10^8\text{ m/s})^2$
$= 24.3 \times 10^{-12}\text{ J} = \mathbf{2.43 \times 10^{-11}\text{ J}}$

PHYSICS GRADE 12

5. $${}^{235}_{92}U + {}^{1}_{0}n \longrightarrow {}^{140}_{54}Xe + {}^{94}_{38}Sr + ?\, {}^{1}_{0}n + \text{energy}$$

How many neutrons are liberated in this fission reaction?

Answer: Subscripts on both sides are equal.

   Superscripts:

$$235 + 1 = 140 + 94 + ?$$
$$236 = 234 + ?$$
$$? = 2$$

Therefore two neutrons are liberated, and the equation is:

$${}^{235}_{92}U + {}^{1}_{0}n \longrightarrow {}^{140}_{54}Xe + {}^{94}_{38}Sr + 2\, {}^{1}_{0}n + \text{energy}$$

Date _____

Invoice Number _____

ORDER FORM

Call or Fax: 1-800-403-4751
www.aestudyguides.com

STUDY GUIDES

BASED ON CANADIAN CURRICULUM

	ISBN	QTY	PRICE	EXTENDED
Math Grade 7	1-55202-054-1		34.95	
Math Grade 8	1-55202-053-3		34.95	
Math Grade 9	1-55202-056-8		34.95	
Math Grade 10 **Pure**	1-55202-110-6		37.95	
Math Grade 11 **Pure**	1-55202-111-4		37.95	
Math Grade 12 **Pure**	1-55202-112-2		37.95	
Math 13/ Math 11 - Intro	1-55202-006-1		34.95	
Math 23 Grade 11	1-55202-047-9		34.95	
Math 33 Grade 12	1-55202-008-8		34.95	
Calculus Grade 12/ University	1-55202-060-6		54.95	
Language Arts Grade 7	1-55202-074-6		34.95	
Language Arts Grade 8	1-55202-075-4		34.95	
Language Arts Grade 9	1-55202-076-2		34.95	
Grammar Basics All Grades	1-55202-077-0		34.95	
English Grade 10	1-55202-078-9		34.95	
English Grade 11	1-55202-079-7		34.95	
English Grade 12	1-55202-080-0		34.95	
Science Grade 7	1-55202-100-9		28.95	
Science Grade 8	1-55202-101-7		28.95	
Science Grade 9	1-55202-102-5		28.95	
Science Grade 10	1-55202-103-3		31.95	
Social Studies/History Grade 7	1-55202-021-5		28.95	
Social Studies/History Grade 8	1-55202-022-3		28.95	
Social Studies/History Grade 9	1-55202-023-1		28.95	
Social Studies/History Grade 10	1-55202-049-5		34.95	
Social Studies/History Grade 11	1-55202-025-8		34.95	
Social Studies/History Grade 12	1-55202-026-6		34.95	
Physics Grade 11	1-55202-027-4		37.95	
Physics Grade 12	1-55202-028-2		37.95	
Biology Grade 11	1-55202-029-0		37.95	
Biology Grade 12	1-55202-030-4		37.95	
Chemistry Grade 11	1-55202-031-2		37.95	
Chemistry Grade 12	1-55202-039-8		37.95	
Shipping-Retail Orders	Subtotal			
1 Study Guide: $ 8.50	Shipping			
Each Additional $ 3.00	GST 7%			
	Total:			

STUDY BUDDY'S
CANADIAN CURRICULUM

	ISBN	QTY	PRICE	EXTENDED
Math Grades 1-6	1-55202-092-4		42.95	
Reading Grades 1-6	1-55202-093-2		31.95	
Spelling Grades 1-6	1-55202-094-0		35.95	
Writing Grades 1-6	1-55202-095-9		37.95	
Science Grades 1-6	1-55202-096-7		32.95	
Social Studies Grades 1-6	1-55202-097-5		35.95	
			Subtotal	
Shipping-Retail Orders				
1 Study Guide: $ 8.50				
Each Additional $ 3.00				
			Shipping	
			GST 7%	
			TOTAL:	

PURCHASER INFORMATION

Name: _____

Address: _____

City: _____ Prov: _____

Postal Code: _____ Phone: _____

Payment Method: (Please check one)
❑ Cheque ❑ Visa ❑ MasterCard

Name on Card: _____

_____

Card #: _____

Exp.: _____ Phone: _____

Signature: _____

_____

SCHOOL PURCHASE ORDER #'S ACCEPTED

Telephone or prepaid orders
may be sent to:

**876 Verdier Avenue
Brentwood Bay, B.C.
V8M 1B9
Phone/Fax 1-800-403-4751**

We Appreciate *Your* Business

05/06

Go Beyond Your Limits With THE ACADEMIC EDGE LTD.